BRAIN TRAINING
for Riders

Unlock Your Riding Potential
with StressLess Techniques for
Conquering Fear, Improving Performance,
and Finding Focused Calm

ANDREA MONSARRAT WALDO

Trafalgar Square
North Pomfret, Vermont

First published in 2016 by
Trafalgar Square Books
North Pomfret, Vermont 05053

Disclaimer of Liability
The author and publisher shall have neither liability nor responsibility to any person or entity with respect to any loss or damage caused or alleged to be caused directly or indirectly by the information contained in this book. While the book is as accurate as the author can make it, there may be errors, omissions, and inaccuracies.

Trafalgar Square Books encourages the use of approved safety helmets in all equestrian sports and activities.

Library of Congress Cataloging-in-Publication Data
Names: Waldo, Andrea, author.
Title: Brain training for riders : unlock your riding potential with stressless
    techniques for conquering fear, improving performance, and finding focused
    calm / Andrea Monsarrat Waldo, MS.
Description: North Pomfret, Vermont : Trafalgar Square Books, 2016. l
    Includes bibliographical references and index.
Identifiers: LCCN 2016024647 (print) l LCCN 2016031886 (ebook) l ISBN
    9781570767517 (pbk.) l ISBN 9781570768163 (Kindle) l ISBN 9781570768170
    (Epub)
Subjects: LCSH: Horsemanship--Psychological aspects.
Classification: LCC SF309 .W226 2016 (print) l LCC SF309 (ebook) l DDC
    798.2--dc23
LC record available at https://lccn.loc.gov/2016024647

Book design by Lauryl Eddlemon
Cover design by RM Didier
Main cover photo by Allan Ajifo/Flickr (aboutmodafinil.com) https://creativecommons.org
    licenses/by/2.0/legalcode; top front left by Jerry O'Neill; top front right and bottom from
    Rookie Reiner and used by permission of the publisher; front middle courtesy of
    Andrea Monsarrat Waldo; back cover by Giuliana Robertson.
Index by Andrea Jones (jonesliteraryservices.com)
Typefaces: Trade Gothic, Calibri

Printed in the United States of America

10 9 8

In memory of my grandmother,
Peggy Monsarrat, who gave me the gift
of horses when I was six years old,

And to my husband, Eric Waldo,
for understanding that I need to ride
as much as I need to breathe.

Contents

Acknowledgments

It may take a village to raise a child, but it takes an entire communion of angels and saints to raise a horsewoman, especially one who decides to write a book on top of everything else.

To my husband, Eric, thank you for, well…everything. Thank you for your wisdom, your humor, your patience with being asked 17 variations of the same question, and most of all for your ability to be the sane, stable one in this relationship. I love you.

To my siblings—my brothers Sean and Alexei, and my sister-in-law Amy—thank you for taking this project seriously from day one, even before I did. Your unfailing enthusiasm, along with ruthless editing of the proposal and early drafts, were invaluable. The random Monty Python quotes, Marvin the Martian videos, and 80s movie references helped too.

Thanks to my mom, Dorothy Monsarrat, for giving me what no one ever gave her: the assurance that I could do anything in this world that I wanted to do. Even horses.

To Sean Coppinger, the family I chose: thanks for 31 years of friendship. You make me remember who I am when I lose my way.

To the other two members of the Triple Combination, Chris Armstrong and Mary Brust: no words. Thank you just doesn't begin to cover it. I can't fathom walking through so much fire, or laughing so hard, with anyone else.

Thank you to my wonderful students and clients, especially those of you who allowed me to share your stories in these pages. This book wouldn't exist without you. It's horribly cliché to say it, but I have learned more from all of you than I have ever taught. I've also laughed harder and longer every day than most people get to do in a year. Thank you all for sharing your real selves with me: the good, the bad, the pretty, the ugly, and the completely hilarious. Your courage astonishes me every single day. I have the best job in the world.

Thanks to Rebecca Didier, Caroline Robbins, Martha Cook, Lila Gendal, and the team at Trafalgar Square Books. You made the process of writing a book feel deceptively smooth, and only mildly terrifying.

Finally, my thanks go to the many horses that have come into my life. You give me great happiness, humility, and sometimes peace; you always challenge me to become more than I am; and you make my life whole.

Introduction

August days don't come any more perfect than this one: warm but not hot, clear skies, a slight breeze. I walked up to the fourth jump on my cross-country course, a green table that looked like it could seat Harry Potter's giant friend Hagrid and his entire family for Thanksgiving dinner. There were four normal-sized people stretched out across the top of it, chatting happily.

I swallowed—actually, it was more of a gulp. I'd been stressing out about this jump for an entire year, ever since it had debuted on last year's course when I had started to contemplate a move up to this level. It hadn't gotten any smaller.

I looked at my coach. "Normal people don't do this. Normal people bake cookies on the weekends."

He just grinned at me. "Or they go to the beach," he suggested helpfully.

"The beach sounds great. Let's go to the beach." I wasn't entirely sure I was kidding.

"Just ride forward and come in straight and strong. It will ride fine." I wondered briefly if I still even owned a bathing suit.

The next day, my Thoroughbred, Chauncy, hopped over the table as if he barely needed to pick up his feet. "Oh, it's going to be a good day," I thought, and pressed on to the next jump. When I crossed the finish line, I was wearing a smile that lasted for the next four days.

I still get a thrill in my chest whenever I think about that day. Nothing in my life compares to the thrill of finishing a challenging cross-country ride, whether it's an imposing course on my upper-level event horse or taking a green youngster around his first baby novice. And yet, when I walk my next course or ride around the dressage ring waiting to start my test, my stomach will still flip over. I'll still wake up on a competition morning, fantasizing about going to the beach instead of facing the stress of the day ahead. The stories in my head start spinning: What if we're not ready? What if I fall off? What if I'm not good enough? What if I don't belong at this level? Who do I think I am, anyway?

I decided a few years ago that since they wouldn't just go away and leave me alone, I needed a way to cope with these frustrating, counter-productive thoughts and feelings. My students and my fellow trainers said that they did, too. I started talking with people in other disciplines—dressage, hunter/jumpers, saddle-seat—and sure enough, they all said the same thing: no matter how much experience and success they had accumulated, coping with stress, anxiety, and pressure was a huge challenge. Colleagues who had conquered the most difficult competitions in the country told me that they still have a voice inside that says, "You're not good enough." And so the idea for this book was born.

> *"I've spent most of my life riding horses.*
> *The rest I've just wasted."* —Unknown

Since you're reading this book, I suspect that you agree with this sentiment! You undoubtedly love horses and love riding to a degree that seems irrational or even obsessive to a lot of other people. Your non-horsey friends probably roll their eyes when you and a fellow equestrian strike up a conversation, because they know they're going to be standing around for awhile.

However, like me, you probably also get stressed, nervous, or anxious sometimes, whether in competition or riding at home. It may feel like these emotions overtake the pleasure you get from your riding and you want to change that. You're tired of the voices in your brain that say, "You can't do this," or "You're too old," or "Watch out, something terrible is going to happen!" You need strategies that will help you become more confident in the saddle and enjoy your riding more.

You also may feel like your brain plays tricks on you in competition situations: your riding skills are there, but you need to sharpen your focus, or you have difficulty quieting the mental chatter in your mind. There are days when you and your horse are in perfect sync, but there are others when you completely forget everything you know and do every single thing you know you're not supposed to do. It's as if your brain completely freezes, like a computer that needs a reboot. Your practice at home is solid, but you aren't sure how to reproduce that level of confidence and quality in a competitive situation.

Maybe you're in the midst of a crisis in your riding, caused by a major accident or injury, or by riding a horse that is damaging your confidence. Your brain won't seem to allow you to get past it; you don't know how to move beyond your current feelings of fear or frustration. You're not sure if you need to adjust your outlook, change your goals, or just sell your horse and find a new partner that suits you better. All you know is that you can't "just get over it."

This book is a how-to manual for your brain. To paraphrase Yogi Berra, riding is "90 percent mental, and the other half is physical." I'm going to show you how to train your brain to handle strong emotions such as fear and doubt, to focus and stay calm under pressure, to produce your best performance when it really counts, and to bounce back from inevitable painful experiences. I call this program StressLess Riding.

I created StressLess Riding sort of by accident. For most of my 20-year career as a riding instructor, I was also a psychotherapist, specializing in solution-focused therapy for problems such as Post-Traumatic Stress Disorder (PTSD), depression, and anxiety. I helped people change thought patterns that were getting in their way and helped them develop skills for managing difficult emotions such as anxiety and frustration. These strategies carried over very naturally into my riding instruction, so discussing worries and self-defeating thoughts became just another part of the lesson, right along with "heels down."

I found that many of my students, especially adults, had tried many sports psychology techniques such as relaxation and visualization exercises, but the techniques hadn't worked for them or they hadn't stuck with them. "I have enough trouble trying to ride while also juggling a family and a job—I don't have another 30 minutes to sit and do visualization exercises," they told me in frustration.

Frankly, I am in the same boat. I've struggled with relaxation and visualization work. I always have good intentions: I settle into a chair and close my eyes, take a few deep breaths. Then I remember that I have to pay the farrier tomorrow, and clean my tack for my lesson. We could have lasagna for dinner; do we have any noodles or do I need to get some? Wow, the dog is snoring really loudly. Should I jump or do flatwork today? Oh, look, there's a hole in my jeans—oops. I was supposed to have my eyes closed. Damn.

You get the picture—this isn't exactly working according to plan. While I know I would improve if I practiced, I always seem to find something more important to do, like wash the truck or watch the cross-country video that the Horse Pesterer just posted on YouTube. I need mental techniques that I can do while I'm riding or grooming my horse or driving somewhere in my car. Anything that involves sitting still is likely to fail in my world. And I don't even have kids; my friends and students who do have children have even less time than I do.

I also have two major problems with the concept of "relaxation" when it pertains to riding. One, it's an emotion, and emotions are notoriously difficult to produce on demand. If it were easy, we'd all be happy and relaxed all of the time! And two, I don't actually think relaxation is the ideal performance state for riding. Calm, yes; focused, yes; supple, yes; but these behaviors take effort, and "relaxation" is too casual a feeling to be included in these mental states. Especially as an event rider, where cross-country jumping reigns supreme, "casual" is not part of my ideal performance self. And regardless of your discipline, it takes constant attention to handle a 1200-pound flight animal with a mind of his own. I prefer to save relaxation for after my ride, when I'm hanging out and chatting in the tack room.

Once I decided to let go of "relaxation" as a primary goal, I still needed techniques that would quiet the mental static in my brain, but ones that kept me sharp and focused. I started reading books about other sports that demand highly focused attention: tennis, golf, even football. I borrowed liberally from them and made up a few tricks of my own. I tried things out in my own riding and used my students as guinea pigs (sorry, guys, now you know!). We kept some things, tossed others, tweaking and adjusting to suit different situations and the personalities of horses and riders. We discovered that humor is one of the best tools ever—walk into my barn on any given day and I might be telling someone to ride like Jack Sparrow (yes, Johnny Depp's *Pirates of the Caribbean* Jack Sparrow) while our farm's other instructor, Mary, extols the virtues of her Wonder Woman cape (see the section on talismans in chapter 6)! Nothing is too strange or too funny, because when laughter is present, fear usually doesn't stick around for very long.

In horse training it's very important to be systematic, but humans all have unique minds and unique riding experiences, so we need mental strategies that are custom-made to suit these qualities. Throughout the book, you'll be encouraged to adapt all of the ideas to suit your particular needs as a rider.

HOW TO USE THIS BOOK

Part I, *StressLess Riding Fundamentals,* covers and explains the following:

• The most common equestrian conundrum: "If I know what I'm sup-posed to do, why do I seem to do the exact *opposite* when I'm nervous?"

• How stress, fear, and anxiety operate in the brain, which helps make sense of those times when you can't think straight, or when you get stuck in a rut of negative thoughts and can't get out.

• How to handle uncomfortable emotions such as anxiety and embar-rassment, to use your self-talk for good instead of evil, and to ride your best regardless of what you're feeling in any given situation.

If you don't have particular struggles with nerves or anxiety and you've bought this book to learn better competition skills, you may be tempted to skip this section but I recommend you read it anyway. The competitive skills in Part II build on the information in Part I. The first chapter on stress and the brain is essential, so at least read this before diving into Part II.

Part II, *Focus, Confidence, and StressLess Performance,* is about more than showing or competing, it's about honing your mental game at home to get the most out of your daily riding. It addresses several important topics from several points of view, including current research and the experience of high-performance athletes in a variety of sports:

• It explains the amazing research going on that delves into what makes elite athletes so much better than everybody else. It turns out that you and I have access to many of the same tools that the greatest riders in the world possess, regardless of the balances in our checkbooks (often low) or the number of world-classes horses in our barns (even lower). Money and excellent horses help, of course, but the real power is in the way the best riders practice on a daily basis—and that is a skill set that anyone can tap into.

• It will demonstrate how to focus your riding time to squeeze out every possible drop of improvement, allowing you to make greater progress even if you can't ride every day.

For *competitors,* Part II offers in-the-moment strategies for building the best performance possible. I'll show you how to:

• Arrange your environment and manage your thinking.

• Produce a state of "Focused Calm."

• Tap into your skills, regardless of your emotional state, to produce an outstanding ride.

Part III, *Battling the Big Demons,* is for riders who are coping with particularly challenging situations.

• Chapter 7 addresses that situation we all wish we could avoid: recovering from a bad fall or other traumatic riding event.

• I show you how to care for your emotional injuries in the same way you would care for your injured horse.

• Chapter 8 looks directly at an issue that many of us have trouble facing: deciding whether we are riding the right horse. Sometimes all the love and good intentions in the world aren't enough to turn the wrong match into a happy marriage, and this chapter will help you decide whether to persevere or move on.

Part IV, StressLess Techniques for Trainers demonstrates:

• How to harness the brain's natural tendencies to help students progress efficiently and effectively.

• Solutions to common struggles we face every day with our students.

As you read this book, take what works and leave the rest: everyone has different riding and learning styles, and what works for one person might not work for another. All of the exercises can be used in any riding discipline. I'm an event rider, so I look at things from the point of view of dressage and jumping, but everything in this book is designed to be useful whether you're in the show ring, on a trail ride, doing team penning, or just strolling bareback down the driveway.

One final but critical point: in order to decide what works, you must do the exercises. Don't just read them and think, "That's not my thing." Time and again I've had students tell me, "When you suggested I do X, I thought it was completely stupid and it would never work. But then I went ahead and tried it, and it actually helped!" I've had the same experience—I've been convinced that something is ridiculous, but it works beautifully, while something else makes perfect sense in theory but is an epic fail in practice.

In addition, remember that training your brain is the same as training your body: you need to practice regularly. No skill or technique in the world will work properly if you only try to use it in high-pressure situations. Brain training needs to become an integral part of your riding practice in order to be effective. I've made most of the exercises in this book very simple, short, and portable, so that you can incorporate them into your daily riding routine without adding a lot of extra time and effort. Feel free to tweak, twist, and corrupt any or all of these ideas so that they suit your own needs. Even better, share the new permutations on the StressLess Riding Facebook page so the rest of us can learn from your ideas!

Now, get ready for a tour of your brain and a meeting with a certain reptile that has a huge influence on your riding and your life!

PART I

StressLess Riding Fundamentals:
Brain Basics or How to
Train Your Inner Lizard

Your Brain on Stress:
Meet Your Inner Lizard

Another lovely summer day, another cross-country course walk. I stood in front of the cordwood jump, the first sizable fence on my cross-country course, and felt my stomach flip over. Just like that green table I told you about in the Introduction, it looked bigger than anything I'd ever jumped before. (Bet you're sensing a theme here.) I swear it got bigger as I stood there.

As usual, the Committee in my head started yammering: "Can you really handle that? It's huge. What if you miss your takeoff spot? What if you mess up your horse? She's green, remember, and if you scare her, you're going to screw her up for life. You could have a rotational fall and get really hurt—it just happened to a Big Name Rider, it could happen to you—and your family will be watching and your friends will be watching and...." I took a deep breath and slowly blew it out.

"Time to practice what I preach," I thought, and reminded myself, "My horse doesn't care. We jumped bigger on Tuesday." Standing back from the jump again, I repeated my mantra for the course: "Sit up and kick, sit up and kick." It started to look a little less gigantic. I ran my hand across the top of the jump and walked past it. A friend of mine was walking by at that moment. I rolled my eyes at her and said, "Hours and hours of wanting to throw up, all for six minutes of adrenaline rush. We are a sick, twisted bunch of individuals." She laughed and answered, "Yeah, but we can't not do it, can we?" The next morning, as I crossed the finish line grinning, I was reminded of how right she was.

Since you're still reading, I assume that you love to ride; in fact, I'm willing to bet that riding for you is probably equivalent to breathing, or at least to really *living* life. It's not a hobby; it's a way of life. You may have given it up for periods of your life to go to college, start a family, or build your career, only to pick it up again because you couldn't stay away. At least once a day there is a post on my Facebook feed referring to riding as an addiction, an obsession, an all-consuming passion.

And yet you probably have moments like my course-walk experience when you think, "You know, I could just go home and clean the garage like a normal person." Riding may be your greatest joy, but it also stresses you out at times. You may get nervous at shows, or in lessons, or when you jump, or ride outside of the ring. You may be absolutely terrified of cantering across a field. You may be scared of your horse because you feel overwhelmed by his powerful stride, or because you've been tossed by his athletic buck. The feelings may be so intense that your mother, your best friend, or your significant other asks, "Why are you even riding? It just makes you miserable." And yet you keep coming back. You can't *not* keep coming back.

This first chapter explores why riding, this sport we love so much, can also stress us, worry us, even scare us. You'll learn how and why your brain reacts with fear, and why your body and mind respond in certain ways. You'll come to understand that anxiety is not the enemy, and I'll suggest more useful ways of seeing your fearful emotions that will set the stage for increasing your confidence in the saddle and your deep enjoyment of the sport.

WHY DO YOU RIDE?

Whether you ride for pleasure or competition, relaxation or exhilaration, your reasons for riding are uniquely yours. There are no right or wrong reasons, as long as your riding brings you joy. However, when you run into obstacles in riding and become frustrated or discouraged, it's easy to lose sight of what you love about the sport in the first place. The following exercise can help you reconnect with the things that you love about riding and horses. This is the only time I'll ask you to do a visualization exercise! Read all the way through it before beginning the exercise, because it's easier to do with your eyes closed.

 Exercise: Visualization

1 Find a place where you can be alone for at least 10 minutes.

2 Sit comfortably, close your eyes, and take a few deep, slow breaths. As you breathe, allow your outside thoughts to fall away and let yourself settle.

3 Now call to mind one of your favorite memories of riding. Play it through your mind as if it is happening to you now, as if you are inside a movie of the memory.

4 In your mind's eye, look around and notice what you see. Where are you? What color is your horse's coat? His mane? What are you wearing? What season is it, and what is going on around you? Notice all of your surroundings, whether they are passing by quickly or slowly, if you are alone or with others.

5 Feel the sensations of your body: How fast are you traveling? What gait are you in? Is the air warm or cool? Feel your horse moving underneath you, the reins in your fingers, your seat in the saddle or on his bare back.

6 Hear the sounds around you: hoofbeats, your horse's snorts, the creak of your tack, your breathing, the wind in your ears. Are there voices nearby, or sounds of birds or other animals?

7 Breathe in and smell your horse's scent, the air around you, the scent of your tack.

8 Notice your emotions: Are you exhilarated, excited, peaceful? Allow yourself to enjoy the memory all the way until its end, then gently blink your eyes open.

While it's still fresh in your mind, take a notebook, journal, or in notes on your tablet or computer, write down what you experienced and felt inside your memory.

Ultimately, this is why we do this: it's because we want to have these experiences and feel these emotions.

When I lead this exercise in workshops, I watch all kinds of emotions play across people's faces: joy, peace, excitement. There are also people who say that the memory makes them sad because they have lost these joyful feelings and are afraid they won't be able to ever get them back again. If this describes you, the rest of this book will help you regain these emotions and help you love your riding again.

Before we move on, I want you to notice one more thing about this exercise: *absolutely nothing happened just now,* and yet you felt the emotions of that memory as if it were actually occurring. You weren't riding, your horse wasn't here, but *your emotions reacted as if you were actually having that experience. This is extremely important,* and we'll focus on it in detail throughout the book.

WHY DO I *DO* THAT WHEN I'M NERVOUS?

- "When I'm in the warm-up, there's so much static in my head that I can't even hear my trainer."

- "No matter how many times I practice my dressage test, my mind goes blank when the judge rings the bell."

- "At home I'm pretty good at finding my distances to the jumps, but at the show I pick at my horse and my rounds become all herky-jerky. It drives my trainer crazy!"

- "I *know* I should sit up if my horse bucks, but in the moment I lean forward, pinch, and grab his mouth anyway. It's so frustrating!"

Do any of these statements sound familiar? I hear dozens of complaints just like them in my lessons and clinics, and I've voiced many of those same complaints myself. Our behavior when we're stressed, nervous, or scared is often the opposite of what we know we *should* do. Why does this happen? In order to understand this maddening phenomenon, we need to understand how the brain works when we're afraid; to understand the brain, we need to go back to Darwin.

A QUICK TOUR OF THE BRAIN

The human brain has evolved over millions of years. It's now a complex, intricate structure capable of processing staggering amounts of information in the blink of an eye. But at the beginning, it was a much simpler organ. As vertebrates (any creature with a spinal cord) evolved, they developed a *brain stem,* now located at the base of our brain at the back of our head, just above the spinal cord. The brain stem controls the body's "housekeeping" functions: breathing, heartbeat, digestion, and other ongoing processes that keep the body alive.

As evolution continued, we developed the capacity for emotions. The *amygdala*, which sits very near the brain stem, is the part of the brain responsible for these basic emotions: happy, sad, mad, and scared. Nearby is the *hippocampus,* which has a large role in memory.

The area that includes the brain stem and the amygdala is often referred to as the "Lizard Brain" or the "Reptile Brain," because reptiles seem to have been the first animals to possess this area.

Much, much later, we evolved our *prefrontal cortex,* a very large section located just behind the forehead. This is your "Rational Brain," the part of the brain that controls logical thought: it allows you to plan that after you read this chapter, you need to pick up your son from soccer, buy grain, and remind your spouse that tomorrow is recycling day. It also allows you to do cool things like think in the abstract and come up with great inventions like saddles and Velcro and duct tape. We tend to rely on the prefrontal cortex to get us through the day. Twenty-first century Western culture places a heavy value on things like logical thinking, planning, and verbal abilities, so it's usually steering the ship under normal circumstances.

There are many other structures within the brain, but the Lizard Brain and the Rational Brain are the ones that are the most important for our discussion here.

Your Brain on Stress: The Fight or Flight Response

We humans like to view ourselves as rational creatures who make reasoned, logical decisions and choices. Ideally, we want our choices to support our long term goals. But as much as we *know* that an apple is better than a cookie and that paying the electric bill is more important than the tack shop's clearance sale, our Lizard Brain couldn't care less about "long term health" or "financial stability." It thinks only about the immediate moment, and it cares about only one thing in this moment: survival.

Winning the evolution game is about surviving long enough to reproduce and pass on your DNA to the next generation. Up until very recently, humans lived in an environment with lethal threats all around: saber-toothed tigers, poisonous snakes, enemy tribes. Our ancestors that survived long enough to reproduce didn't survive because they avoided fast food and gluten and balanced their checkbooks every week; they survived because their brains developed a mechanism to get them out of danger as fast as possible. This mechanism is known as the Fight or Flight Response (FOFR). Here's how it works:

Imagine you're grooming your horse and you're leaning over to brush mud off his belly. Suddenly he kicks up at a fly and you jump out of the way just in time to avoid being kicked yourself. You realize he came dangerously close to nailing you right in the head! Now imagine how you feel: your stomach is quivering, your heart is pounding, your hands are shaking a little, and every muscle is tense. You've just been protected by your FOFR.

Remember the *amygdala*? Think of it as your body's alarm system. When your brain perceives a threat in the environment, the amygdala signals the brain to engage the FOFR. A surge of stress hormones, primarily adrenaline and cortisol, are released into your bloodstream and trigger a rapid series of physiological changes. Your heart beats faster to get more blood to the major muscle groups in your arms and legs, which tense up to prepare to fight or run. You breathe faster to get more oxygen into your bloodstream. You start to perspire. Blood is channeled away from your extremities and momentarily unnecessary organs such as your stomach.

This is why you may get cold hands and butterflies in your stomach when you're nervous, and why you have such a hard time relaxing your muscles enough to deepen your seat and stay tall in the saddle.

An important point to note here is that the FOFR can activate when it perceives *any* threat. It responds whether that threat is physical, such as a kick from a horse, or psychological, such as the worry that you'll forget your reining pattern. It also gets activated *whether the perceived threat is real or imagined.* This is why you can feel jittery just picturing your horse bucking you off.

Remember how you felt those wonderful emotions in response to your favorite memory of your horse? Your brain responded to the memory by creating real emotions, experienced in the present moment, even though they were triggered by your imagination, and not by an actual present-moment experience. The Lizard Brain can't tell the difference between something you imagine vividly and something that's actually happening.

On the positive side, you can feel great when you imagine something wonderful; on the down side, you can panic your Lizard Brain by picturing something terrible happening. You can also make your Lizard Brain angry (the fight in Fight or Flight) by imagining a conflict. (Ever re-live an argument with your significant other in your mind and find yourself angry all over again? Hello, Lizard Brain!)

One more interesting thing happens during the FOFR. The *prefrontal cortex*—the Rational Brain that thinks things through logically—*shuts down.* It's never even consulted in the Fight or Flight process. It's as if you were flying over southern California at night, and all of a sudden, Los Angeles went totally dark. The FOFR flips a switch, and off goes your Rational Brain.

At first glance, this may seem like an evolutionary design flaw. Why on earth would you want your logical thinking capacity disconnected? However, it makes sense when you look at it from a survival perspective: Imagine you're a caveman a hundred thousand years ago. One morning, you stroll out of your cave and spy a saber-toothed tiger stalking in the bushes. Your Rational prefrontal cortex might say something like this: "Oh, hey, a tiger. Or is it a lion? Nope, it has saber teeth, definitely a tiger. What should I do? I could hit it with my club—no, that's in the cave. I could climb that tree or hide behind that rock, but it might find me. I guess I'd better run—" CHOMP!

By now, the tiger has finished his delightful lunch of cave-human. In life-or-death situations, reasoning and logic simply take too much time. Instead, the amygdala hollers, "TIGER! RUN!" and you live to see another day.

This, dear rider, is why you can't think straight when you're extremely nervous: your amygdala has hijacked your Rational Brain. You're not stupid or inept; you've just allowed your Lizard Brain to run the show. It thinks you're being attacked by a tiger, so it tries to get you to safety.

I mentioned earlier that the Lizard Brain can't distinguish between a psychological threat and a physical one; it uses the same response for both. This is why a dressage judge can send your heart pounding and wipe your brain clean of everything you knew five minutes ago.

My Lizard Brain is why my stomach started doing acrobatics when I simply thought about jumping that big cordwood on my cross-country course. To the Lizard Brain, a threat is a threat, and you either need to kill it or run away from it as fast as possible. It doesn't see any other alternatives. This in an unfortunate reality of evolution: it moves much, much more slowly than our cultural development has done.

In the last 200 years or so we have eliminated nearly all of the daily *physical* threats that plagued our ancestors. In their place, *psychological* stressors such as financial concerns and fear of emotional rejection have grown instead. However, the human brain has not evolved to keep up with this rapid shift, so we're stuck with the FOFR as our instinctive reaction to stress of any kind. Fortunately, there *are* ways of managing the FOFR and regaining control of your thinking, and I'll discuss them throughout the remainder of this book.

Instinctive Reactions vs. Effective Responses

Another physical response to anxiety needs to be mentioned here: the tendency to tense up and lean forward, especially when you feel like you're going to fall off your horse. We all know it's wrong, but we all do it at least some of the time. Why would we do something that's the complete opposite of what we know to be right? Again, the answer is survival. Babies are born with very few fears, but one of them is the fear of falling. Humans are born with a reflex to protect ourselves during a fall: we curl up into the fetal position. We literally spend nine months practicing before we even join the outside world! The fetal position does a brilliant job of protecting our inner organs *once we are already falling*; it just doesn't help us when we want to prevent the fall in the first place. In order to ride well, then, we actually have to override our most ancient instinct. It's pretty amazing that we're actually successful most of the time!

"Excuse Me, But Who Thought *This* Was a Good Idea?"

Many people get a bit exasperated with me at this point. "But Andrea, I love to ride and I know how to do things correctly in the saddle. I've had hours, even years of experience. So why do I still get freaked out at random times by something I know how to do, and that I love so much?"

The answer goes back to slow evolution and the Lizard Brain, which doesn't share our Rational Brain's love of logic. Look at it from your Lizard's point of view for a moment: you want to climb up on a 1000-pound creature so that your head, with its soft, fragile brain, is seven feet or more from the ground. The creature is a flight animal that runs away first (really fast) and asks questions later. You're going to ask this creature to carry you over all kinds of terrain at speeds of up to 20 or 30 miles per hour. You might even make it chase after other animals or jump over obstacles that may not fall down when you hit them. If you're

MY STORY: **THE LIZARD COMES WITH THE TERRITORY**

I had a huge epiphany about 10 years into my riding career. I was warming up for the cross-country phase at my second Preliminary level event and I was incredibly nervous. The water jump, a maximum-sized bank down into the water with a narrow jump on the way out, was especially sending my stomach into triple flips—it looked like I was jumping off the edge of the world.

My Lizard Brain was absolutely convinced that I was going to crash and die. Then, when I was only two riders away from going into the start box, the officials called a hold in the competition and told us there would be at least a 45-minute delay. Right after that, the ambulance drove out onto the course! Needless to say, my Lizard Brain went into an absolute frenzy. It was sure we were doomed.

My jumping trainer at the time, Denny Emerson, happened to be riding in the same division. For those who don't know him, Denny is one of eventing's "old guard," and at the time of this writing has been competing for over 60 years in multiple equestrian disciplines. He knows his stuff. I went to him with a sense of desperation and asked, "Okay, Denny, you've been doing this longer than any of us. When do you stop wanting to throw up before you go into the start box?" He just snorted and shrugged. "Never," he answered.

I tell this story at all of my workshops, and at this point someone always exclaims, "Oh great! I'm stuck with this forever!" My reaction, though, was a wave of relief. "Oh, thank goodness," I thought, "there's nothing wrong with me!" I realized that if Denny still feels this way after six decades, then it is just part of the deal. That sick feeling doesn't mean that I'm unprepared or that something terrible is going to happen, it's just my brain telling my body to gear up for a tough challenge. That experience completely revolutionized my relationship to my start-box anxiety. I still get nervous, but I no longer get nervous about being nervous! I just think, "Oh yuck, there's that sick feeling. That always happens. It'll go away once I get out on the course." I've eliminated an entire level of stress with this outlook.

really smart, you'll do all of this with a plastic bowl on your head for protection. You do all of this just for fun.

Now can you see why the Lizard is freaking out?

How Does This Help?

Understanding how your brain works is incredibly helpful when you get nervous or stressed. It allows you to stop judging yourself for feeling the way you feel—after all, you're not going to change millions of years of evolution simply by willing yourself to "just relax." It also allows you to step back and reactivate your higher level thinking so you can be objective instead of getting swept away by your emotions.

When you feel your heart pounding and your muscles tensing, you can say, "That's just my FOFR—my brain thinks I'm about to get eaten by a tiger. I'm just fine at the moment, though, and now I need to decide what I can do to make the situation better." It helps you regain control of the ride instead of being hijacked by your amygdala.

How Do I Get Rid of This Lizard Thing?

Riders often ask me how they can shut down their FOFR. The truth is that you can't get rid of it, at least not entirely. And you wouldn't really want to, especially if your equestrian discipline includes high risk activities such as jumping or bronc riding. Anxiety at moderate levels helps keep you sharp and alert, able to respond quickly without the need for much time-consuming verbal and logical thought.

The feeling of motivation is a type of anxiety as well, one that helps you stay on track in pursuit of your goals. So I'm afraid that nowhere in the rest of this book will you find a way to eliminate stress, fear, anxiety, or nervousness from your riding or your life. Instead, I will show you how to bring those emotions down to a manageable size so that you can ride well and enjoy yourself regardless of your feelings in the moment. We'll get started on this process right away in chapter 2.

You will learn a set of skills that will help your higher-level thinking take the reins back from the Lizard Brain. Just as you teach your horse to remain calm in the presence of scary experiences such as barking dogs or big trucks rolling noisily by, you can train yourself to be calm when your own FOFR wants to take over.

IT WORKS IF YOU DO IT

Most of the riders I know understand the importance of training and conditioning their horses. They take lessons and practice what they learn. *StressLess Riding* is a *mental training program.* It's not a one-shot fix and it's not something you can just read about if you want to see real results in your riding. If such a thing exists, no one I know has discovered it yet.

To see real results, make sure you actually do the exercises throughout this book. Try them, and then practice them as regularly as you practice your position in the saddle. All of them can be practiced while you are with your horse, either riding or grooming. Many of them also can be practiced while you're doing other things—folding laundry, washing dishes, or eating lunch at work. Just as posting the trot or following the canter got easier as you practiced, the techniques in the following chapters will become second nature with repetition and time. Before you know it, those saber-toothed tigers won't seem so threatening anymore.

Stress Less:
Don't Let the Lizard Hold the Reins

CONTROLLING YOUR FIGHT OR FLIGHT RESPONSE

Now that you understand how your brain's fear response operates and why it does what it does, you can focus on how to prevent that fear from getting so big that it hijacks your ride. Before I offer suggestions for what to do, I'll tell you what not to do: don't tell it to shut up and go away. Don't pretend that it doesn't exist. Don't tell your fear that it's stupid or ridiculous and it shouldn't be there.

Remember, fear is your body's alarm system, its way of telling you that SOMETHING IS VERY WRONG. Alarms don't stop if you ignore them; they just keep on sounding until you do something about them. Human alarm systems even have an escalation feature built in. Think about this: if you see a small child running toward a busy street, what do you do? You shout at him to stop. If he doesn't listen, you shout louder, and if that doesn't work, you run and grab him!

All of this happens in a matter of seconds—if not less. Your FOFR can escalate in the same way, rapidly intensifying your feelings of fear until it gets your attention. Covering your ears and repeating "Not listening! Not listening!" just doesn't work. So what should you do instead?

Recognition

This may sound obvious, but the first step in managing your nerves is to realize that they are there in the first place. People experience anxiety in different ways, depending on their temperament and past experiences. Some people get restless and pace a lot ("flight"), while others get irritable and snap at the people around them ("fight"). Others seem like a deer in the headlights ("freeze," another way of fleeing) and can't respond to anything around them. Some people start micromanaging their environment, which often includes their horses, usually with poor results. A few of my students can't stop talking, and some of them stop talking altogether—when these two types are sharing a trailer at a show, it often doesn't go very well!

The inner experience of anxiety differs from person to person as well. Some riders feel their mind go blank, while others hear incessant chatter in their head. While one rider becomes very tense and rigid, another may become floppy and physically disorganized. Stomach upset and inability to eat are common experiences.

Exercise: Recognize Your FOFR

List your internal and external signs of worry, anxiety, or nervousness. If you aren't sure how you express these signs (feeling or behavior) outwardly, ask someone close to you. I asked my business partner this question and she said, "Your sentences get shorter." I had no idea.

When you notice any of these feelings or behaviors, label them: "Oh look, that's me getting nervous." Labeling how you feel helps you take a step back from the emotion so that you're not swamped by it. Do this out loud if you can—hearing yourself say it out loud is more powerful than just thinking it inside your head. Plus, if you're talking, you're usually breathing, and that will help to slow your FOFR as well.

In order to cope effectively with your nerves, it's important to recognize how they express themselves, both internally and to the outside world. This is especially true if you tend to mask anxiety with anger or irritability. This is usually the brain preferring "fight" to "flight"—it feels more powerful. However, it's detrimental to your relationship with your horse and with the people around you.

Breathe!

Speaking of breathing: if you're in the middle of Fight or Flight, chances are good that you're either holding your breath or breathing fast and shallow. You need to start breathing correctly in order to slow your FOFR. Take a deep breath, and notice: did your shoulders come up and your upper chest expand? If so, you're not truly breathing deeply. Instead, take a "soup breath": breathe in slowly, to at least a count of four, all the way down into your lungs so that your stomach expands like a balloon.

Now, purse your lips and blow out slowly through your mouth, as if you're blowing on your soup to cool it. This slows your breath and your heart rate, which then begins to turn down the volume on your FOFR. It also helps your Rational Brain to re-engage, making it easier to think clearly and make better decisions.

Acceptance

The next step in managing fear and anxiety is both acknowledging them and accepting their presence. Most of my students hate this step and often misunderstand it as a form of giving up. "I can't accept my fear, I hate it! I just want it gone! If I give in to it I'll never feel better!" But acceptance doesn't mean liking the feeling or capitulating to it. It simply means saying, "Oh, hi, there you are. I see you." That's all. You're just acknowledging reality as it already exists instead of protesting against it or pretending it isn't so.

This is actually harder than it sounds—Buddhists often call it "radical" acceptance—because denial is much easier in the short term.

We would much rather pretend that everything is fine. That doesn't make the anxiety go away, though; as I mentioned before, it usually makes it kick into high gear because your Lizard Brain is sure that if you ignore it, something terrible is going to happen. But once you simply accept that the nerves are there, you take away one layer of struggle and free up a great deal of mental energy to do something about them. "Oh, it's you. You always insist on showing up, don't you? Okay, now that you're here, I have to figure out what to do with you."

An important point: you'll notice that I'm referring to anxiety or fear as if it's a thing or a person, rather than saying "I am nervous." This is called externalizing, and it's a very handy trick. When you describe a problem as a thing or person, you've separated it from yourself; you've made the problem the problem, instead of making yourself the problem. This makes it feel less like a character defect and more like a puzzle to solve.

If you're a visual learner, you can picture the emotion as a particular creature or object. I tend to use the image of a small lizard, since fear comes from the Lizard Brain. Plus, I think lizards are kind of cute, so it feels less like something I want to squash and more like something I want to take care of. The Pixar movie *Inside Out* also has a great depiction of fear: he's a skinny, neurotic little guy who's always flipping out, but is really quite loveable and is just trying to help. Externalizing may sound a little ridiculous, but I encourage you to try it, because it really does work.

What Are You Afraid Of, Really?

Once you've accepted that a fear is present, you need to understand it. In other words, what are you really afraid of? Often your initial answer to this question is not the only answer or the truest answer. Fear tends to be a multilayered thing, with deeper feelings hiding underneath the surface. When you can mine down under those surface fears and get to the real cause of your anxiety, it's much easier to address it effectively. You do that mining by asking yourself, "What makes that so terrible?"

Here's an example: I had an ugly fall at a cross-country jump a few years ago. My horse hit a fence with her chest, nearly somersaulting over it, and I went flying over the jump and skidding across the grass on the other side. Fortunately we were both okay, but it was a close call. When I had to go back and do that jump again the following year, I was really nervous. My conversation with my fear went something like this:

Fear: I'm really scared of that jump. What if we fall again?

Me: Well, what would make that so terrible?

Fear: Duh, I could get hurt. Or my horse could get hurt this time.

Me: And what would make that so terrible? (Note: stay with me. This is not as stupid a question as it sounds.)

Fear: I might not be able to ride again for a long time, and I love it more than anything. Plus I make my living riding and I might not be able to work.

Me: Okay. Anything else?

Fear: I would feel so guilty if my horse got hurt. She gives me so much; I owe it to her to give her a good ride.

Me: Fair enough. Anything else?

Fear: Everyone knows I fell at that jump last year.

Me: And what makes that so terrible?

Fear: They will think that I can't ride, that I don't belong at that level, that I'm one of those crazy dangerous eventers who don't care about their horse's well-being.

Me: Anything else?

Fear: (Thinks for a while) No, that's the biggie. I want so much to be a good trainer and to have people respect me for having strong skills and good judgment.

Aha. Bull's eye. That was my real fear: that if I fell, it would mean that I wasn't a good trainer. Once I understood this, I could move on to the next step. If I had skipped this step, though, I could have just glossed the problem over with "I've practiced that jump a lot since then and it will be fine," but my real fear would still be there, getting in my way. It's worth it to take the time to understand what you're truly worried about.

 ## Exercise: What Are You Really Afraid Of?

With pen and paper or your tablet, choose a particular stress, worry, or anxiety that has been nagging at you. Have a conversation with your fear like the one above. Ask it, "What makes that so terrible?" Write down everything that comes to mind, no matter how ridiculous or illogical it sounds; remember, fear comes from the Lizard Brain, not the Rational Brain.

Once you get to the end of a fear, ask it, "Is there anything else?" If there is, ask it, "What makes that so terrible?" If nothing else pops up, you've probably found the core fear (there's usually an "aha" feeling that goes along with finding the core fear).

Once you've identified your core worry, it needs two things to be able to step back out of your way: A) Reassurance and B) a Plan.

Reassurance: It's Okay, It's Not a Saber-Toothed Tiger

In chapter 1, I told you that the brain's number one concern is survival, and that fear developed to facilitate that survival. In order to get out of your way, your fear needs to know that you're going to survive whatever is happening; it needs reassurance. "But I've tried that," most people tell me. "I try to tell myself not to worry, that everything's going to be fine, but it doesn't help." That's because those phrases aren't actually reassurance—they're more like dismissal. They carry the underlying message, "You shouldn't feel this way and there's something wrong with you if you do."

Meanwhile, your Lizard Brain is shouting, "LIAR! It's dangerous out there! You don't know that everything's going to be fine!" And your Lizard is right: you can't predict the future, and there is some element of risk every time you get on a horse. While your Lizard Brain does need to accept this element, you can reassure it that in all likelihood you will survive the situation it fears. When it knows you will survive, it can quiet down. Using the example of my fear of falling and losing face with other riders and trainers, here's how to reassure your Lizard Brain.

Fear: If I fall off at that jump again, everyone will think I'm a terrible rider.

Me: Is that thought true?

Fear: Yup. I'm sure of it. (Fear is always sure of everything it believes.)

Me: When we've fallen off before, how did other people react?

Fear: They asked if I was okay. Some people told me they'd fallen at that same fence. Pretty much everyone was really sympathetic. BUT maybe they were just being nice, and they secretly thought I was a terrible rider.

Me: Maybe. But when other people fall, do you think they're terrible riders?

Fear: Not unless I've seen them do something really wrong that caused the fall, and even then I usually think that everyone makes mistakes. I'd only think they were terrible if I'd seen them have the same kind of fall over and over a whole bunch of times, without trying to fix the problem.

Me: So chances are, if you did fall, people would be sympathetic rather than critical.

Fear: Yeah, I guess. BUT some people might still think I'm an idiot to make the same mistake twice.

Me: They might. Could you live with that?

Fear: No, that would be AWFUL! It would be the worst thing ever! I hate it when people think bad things about me. I would just die!

Me: Okay, it would feel terrible. But no one has ever died of embarrassment. So could you live with it?

Fear: (sulking) Yes, it would feel terrible, but I could live with it. I guess it wouldn't kill me.

Remember when I said in chapter 1 that the brain can't tell the difference between a real threat and an imagined one, and that it sees a dressage judge and a saber-toothed tiger as equally threatening? This is why the above conversation is so important. Your fear needs to be reassured that even though something might be difficult, painful or unpleasant, it probably won't be fatal. Reassurance isn't telling yourself that you don't care or that it won't hurt, because that's not always true. It's reminding yourself that even if it feels awful, you can live with it. That's all your fear needs to know in order to feel reassured.

A Plan: Escaping From Tigers

Fears, worries, and anxieties are essentially "what if?" questions. The problem is that we either don't answer the question or we answer it with a worst-case scenario, so we can't imagine a positive outcome. The only outcome we can see when we're afraid of being attacked by a tiger is being eaten by the tiger. Coming up with a plan to solve the "what if" lets the Lizard know that you have a strategy for escaping when the tiger comes out of the woods. When your Lizard Brain needs a plan, ask the following questions:

1 What skills, abilities, or knowledge do I have that will make that worst-case outcome unlikely?

2 What will I do to prevent the situation from happening?

3 If the problem starts to occur, what will I do to solve it?

In the case of my fear of falling at the cross-country jump, the answers look like this:

1 I now know to think about how the time of day will affect the light around the jump (a shadow created the problem that led to the original fall). I've practiced this type of jump repeatedly, so my horse and I are familiar with it.

2 I'll approach the jump with the right pace and balance. I'll set up a few strides earlier than usual to really make sure we get it right.

3 If I feel like I'm going to get to the wrong take-off spot, I'll half-halt to add a stride. If I'm really not sure, I can circle away from the jump and re-approach—it would mean 20 penalties, but 20 points is better than falling. I can also take the option fence if there is one.

Reviewing in detail how to solve the problem will ease your fears and remind you that you have some control over the problem. Now your fear can step back out of the way so you can get on with your ride. Sometimes the plan will involve accessing your physical riding skills;

sometimes it might involve other things, such as successfully resolving a conflict with your trainer or making a decision to ignore someone's critical remarks.

Exercise: Reassuring Your Fear

Offer your fear some reassurance that you will survive if the feared situation occurs. Some helpful questions to ask yourself are:

1 Is this thought true? Is it always true, or does it happen differently sometimes?

2 Is that likely to happen? What's the most likely thing that would happen?

3 If this happened to someone else, what would you think about her and the situation?

4 How has this situation played out in the past? Did the worst case scenario come true?

5 If it does come true, can you live with that? (The answer to this is nearly always "yes.")

What If I'm Still Stuck?

"But what if I can't come up with a plan?" I've been asked. If your answer to the three questions above is "I have no idea," then you don't have a fear problem, you have a training or skills problem. If I didn't know how to get myself out of trouble at this jump, I'd practice it with my trainer until I felt comfortable handling it. If it was too late to do this because I was already at the event, I'd consider withdrawing from the competition—it wouldn't be worth it to risk getting hurt or hurting my horse. My plan at this point would become, "I'm going to seek help dealing with this training problem."

Sometimes the problem isn't with your riding skills; it's that you don't know how to handle a psychological or interpersonal problem, such as how to respond if your trainer yells at you. In this case, ask for input or support from others, or get some training in conflict resolution.

We Can't Control Everything

When teaching this skill, someone always says, "But what if you really do crash and get paralyzed or killed? It could happen." Yes, it could. Despite our best efforts, bad things do happen sometimes. This is especially true with horses, as they're unpredictable flight animals with minds of their own. There will always be elements of a situation that are beyond your control. But, you can give yourself a whopping panic attack if you choose to focus on these elements. If your goal is to manage your fear and become more confident, however, you need to accept that you cannot control everything and that risk is simply part of riding (and life for that matter). When a "what if" is beyond your control, practice saying, "I can't change that, so I choose to let it go." I usually do better with acceptance if I can throw in some humor or sarcasm, so I tell myself, "Drop it. That one is above your pay grade." Someone else I know just says "whatever" in her best annoyed teenager voice. You can come up with a phrase that works for you.

Keep in mind that your brain takes survival so seriously that it has made fear an obnoxiously persistent emotion. Even after you've gone through these steps, it's likely to pop up again. This is irritating, but completely normal. When it happens, reassure it again, remind it of your plan, and then ask it to step out of the way. Repetition is the key with emotional training in much the same way as it is with horse training: the more you do it, the easier it will get, but you have to repeat it many times.

Exercise: Develop a Plan

Using the problem situation from the exercise on page 30 ("What Are You Really Afraid Of?"), write down a plan for how you will prevent the problem from happening and how you will cope with it if it does happen. If your fear says "Yes but," answer those concerns as well. If the "yes but" is beyond your control, come up with a phrase that means "I accept that and I'm letting it go."

CONFIDENCE MEANS OWNING YOUR ABILITIES

Okay, enough talk about fear and doubt for a while. Let's talk about confidence.

Exercise: What Do You Know How to Do?

List 10 of your riding skills.

How hard was this exercise? Did you come up with ten or did you give up somewhere around four? Did you list things like "I can post at the trot" or "I know how to mount properly"? Those are skills that you possess. Every single one counts. Did you say to yourself, "I can do X, but that doesn't really count" or "Any moron can do that" or "I still mess up at that sometimes" or "I'm not as good as so-and-so"? Did you feel embarrassed because it seemed like bragging?

I do this exercise at all of my workshops. I used to ask for 20 skills, but no one could do it. And the actual ability of the rider made no difference in whether they could fill the list. I once gave this exercise to a group that included all levels from beginner riders just learning to canter to a rider who had successfully ridden at the Olympic level. The Olympic rider actually had a harder time coming up with 10 skills than the others did! What is going on here?

If You Can't See It, You Can't Feel It

Do you know anyone who is beautiful—not just pretty, but really gorgeous? Most of us do. And does that person think she's gorgeous? I'll bet she doesn't. And the sad thing is that she'll never feel good about her looks if she can't see herself the way others do. Riders who lack confidence are the same way: they don't recognize their abilities, so they can't possibly have confidence in them. And when they don't have confidence in their abilities, they ride as if they don't have those abilities! I have a riding instructor colleague who says, "Confidence comes from competence." I believe this is true, but I would amend that to say, "Confidence comes from competence and your awareness of that competence." In order to feel sure of yourself, you must own your abilities.

What do I mean by "own your abilities?" When you own something, you claim it as yours: it belongs to you. When you say, "I can do a really good sliding stop," you take possession of that skill, and it becomes part of your identity, part of your self-image as a rider. You're not hedging, you're not downplaying it; you're saying, "Yes, this is a skill that belongs to me." It is an incredibly powerful confidence-builder.

Owning our abilities seems to be a problem for women in particular. (I'm not able to speak for men—someone else will have to write that segment!) From the time that we're small, we're taught to downplay our abilities lest we appear arrogant or make someone else feel bad. One of the worst things one girl can say about another is, "She's so stuck up, she thinks she's all that." Confidence has gotten all mixed up with arrogance and being stuck up, thinking we're "all that."

As a result, we downplay our abilities and exaggerate our weaknesses. If someone gives us a compliment, we usually dismiss or minimize it. For example, one of my students was admiring another rider's leg position. That rider's response? "Oh, but as soon as the jumps get bigger, I'm all over the place!" She couldn't accept the compliment, and as a result, she couldn't see herself as having a good leg. She completely missed out on a chance to feel more confident about her abilities (more on this in the Brain Traps section in chapter 3, p. 50).

Owning your abilities is not the same as bragging. Bragging is usually done to make someone else feel smaller. Recognizing your competence, on the other hand, isn't about comparing yourself to others; instead it allows you to face riding challenges with the knowledge that you are prepared to deal with them.

Many students tell me they're not good at a skill because they don't do it perfectly, or someone else does it better than they do. This misses the point. You don't have to be perfect at something to know how to do it, and you don't have to be the best to be good at it. New Zealand event rider Mark Todd was named Horseman of the Century by *The Chronicle of the Horse,* a major equestrian publication. He has won nearly every major event in the world and has several Olympic medals to his credit. He jumped around Badminton, one of the world's biggest cross-country courses, *with only one stirrup after the other one broke.* Is he perfect? Far from it. He's had many losses, plenty of falls, disastrous dressage tests and piles of rails down in showjumping. Yet there's no denying he's an incredible horseman.

In the same way, we mere mortals don't have to be perfect in order to be skillful. If you can sit the trot without bouncing most of the time on most of the horses you ride, you have good sitting-trot skills. You don't have to wait until it's perfect to move up to the next level; otherwise, everyone would still be doing Introductory Level.

If you can jump a 2'6" fence from the correct distance with a correct position a lot of the time, you're a good 2'6" jumper. Can someone else jump 4'6"? Of course. But that doesn't mean you don't possess the skill, it just means you still have something to strive for. When you acknowledge that you can jump 2'6" well, you'll feel more confident about jumping something bigger, rather than telling yourself that you're not a good jumper because you "only jump 2'6." All skills are works in progress,

LILA'S STORY: **OWN IT**

My friend Lila is one of the most beautiful riders I know. Unbeknownst to her, when she goes into the show ring, people always make comments like "Wow, I wish I could ride like that. Her seat is amazing."

Recently, Lila was riding some horses for another friend of ours. "It seems like everyone at that barn rides each other's horses," she said. "People keep telling me they're excited for me to ride their horse."

I had to laugh. "They're not excited for just anyone to ride their horse. They're excited for you to ride their horse," I told her.

"I don't think it has anything to do with me in particular," she countered. "I think it's just what they do there."

This was not the first time I'd heard Lila discount her considerable skills. "Lila, trust me, people watch you, and they want to ride like you." She started to answer, so I cut her off. "Now's the time when you say 'thank you' and shut up," I teased her.

"Thank you," she muttered. We laughed about it, but I hope she knew I was completely serious: she's a wonderful rider, and she should own it. (By the way, I wasn't being mean by telling her to shut up; she knows my work, so she knew exactly what I was talking about. More about, "Say thank you and shut up" in chapter 3.)

and the best riders are the ones who never stop working on them.

When riders have trouble coming up with a list of their skills, they often take many things for granted. This is especially true of more advanced riders. I pointed out to one lifelong foxhunter that he knows how to gallop downhill. His response was, "That's no big deal, anyone can do that." I had to remind him that many other horse people think foxhunters are completely crazy for galloping downhill! Every skill counts and allows you to build more to move to the next level. Mounting correctly is essential for being able to ride at all! That's easy? It is now, perhaps, but it probably wasn't when you first learned to do it, and if you pulled a non-rider off the street, I guarantee they wouldn't do it correctly.

Another benefit of knowing your strengths is focusing your training in the right direction: you work on what actually needs work, instead of revisiting the same things over and over. A student recently came into a lesson and said she wanted to work on keeping her heels down. After she rode a few circles, I pointed out that her heels were very good and that I hadn't had to remind her to keep them down in quite a while. Instead we shifted the focus of the lesson to her contact with the bit, which did need work. If she had been working on her own, she might have spent a lot of time focusing on something that didn't really need a lot of improvement and she would have missed an opportunity to improve in other areas. Given how precious your time is and how hard you probably work to find time to ride at all, it makes sense to know what is going well and what needs work so you're using your time effectively!

If all of this hasn't convinced you to own your abilities, do it for the sake of your horse. Our horses see us as the leader of their herd, so they look to us for feelings of safety. If we ride timidly and lack confidence in our skills, they will respond with tension and fear: "Whoa! What? Where's the tiger? If you're scared of going across that bridge over that stream, there's no way I'm going over it!" They need us to be sure of ourselves in order to do what we ask of them.

If you aren't sure what you're good at, ask people who see you ride—a trainer, a friend. Ask them to be honest, and listen to their answers without discounting them. Gain more perspective by keeping track of your progress. Each day that you ride, write down what you did correctly—not perfectly, just correctly. Think back to where you were a year ago as a rider, and compare that to what you are doing now. Notice progress, and your confidence will grow accordingly.

Now go back to the beginning of this section (p. 36) and complete your list of 10 riding skills. Hopefully it will be easier this time—but if not, keep practicing!

Watch Your Language!
How Self-Talk Can Hurt or Help Your Riding

NEGATIVE SELF-TALK: ARE YOU YOUR OWN WORST CRITIC?

Everyone talks to themselves. We all have voices in our heads, sometimes just our own, more often an entire committee, narrating and critiquing and commenting on our experiences. In general there's nothing wrong with this; it helps us make sense of our world. But like all of the brain's abilities, this power can be used for good or for evil! Confident riders have learned to use their self-talk to become stronger, more confident, more successful. They are as disciplined about their thinking as they are about their leg position. Many people, however, find themselves sabotaged by the committee in their head that seems to do nothing but criticize and doubt them. They are at the mercy of their Negative Self-Talk (NST). Recognizing and changing negative thought patterns is a critical foundation skill for becoming confident in your riding (and anywhere else in life, for that matter).

• "You should just sell your horse and quit riding. You're never going to get any better so you might as well just give up."

• "Everyone else here is better than you. You have no business being here. What made you think you could compete against these pros when you're just a hack?"

• "You're such a wimp. No one else is scared of that jump."

• "You're worse than a worm. You're the worm at the bottom of the manure pile."

These statements sound like the script for *Mean Girls Go to the Horse Show.* But these weren't said by one teenaged girl to another. These are actual quotes that some of my clients say to themselves, both inside their heads and out loud. Actually, the second one is from my own head, and I did *not* make that last one up. While negative comments from others can be hurtful, NST is even more destructive because it's the self attacking the self. All the praise and accolades in the world can be silenced instantly by a cutting remark from our own brain. NST cuts us off at the knees before we ever get started, and it can sabotage even the biggest success.

What's so bad about NST? Imagine hearing an adult in a grocery store yelling at a child, "You pathetic idiot, I can't believe you dropped the milk! How could you be so stupid and clumsy?" How would you feel witnessing this? Probably disturbed, at the very least. Most people know intuitively that if you tell a small child something often enough, they will eventually believe it. It's upsetting when someone constantly criticizes a child because we know that eventually she will believe that she is worthless or incompetent.

The same thing happens to adults, though, when we criticize ourselves relentlessly. What you say and believe about yourself directly affects how you feel and act. If you tell yourself, "I'm a terrible rider," you are likely to approach a jump less confidently than if you think, "I know how to do this." That tentative approach may lead to a poor

MICHAELA'S STORY: **WHEN NST RUNS THE SHOW**

I had a gifted, hard-working student a few years back; I'll call her Michaela. She was 15, and had a pretty, talented, but difficult mare named Lucy. Michaela also had a father who thought the best way to motivate his daughter to succeed was to tell her she couldn't do things: she wasn't as good at math as her brother, she didn't play soccer as well as her younger sister, she wasn't as athletic as her classmate, Megan. "He says he does that because he wants me to get so mad at him that I'll prove him wrong," she confessed to me after I witnessed one of these interactions.

Unfortunately, Michaela never got as angry at her dad as she did at herself; she clearly had internalized her father's messages, and she was at the mercy of her Negative Self-Talk. Any time Lucy acted up or didn't cooperate (which was often), Michaela blamed herself. "I suck. A monkey could ride this horse better than I can," she would tell me in shame and frustration. The more she talked to herself like this, the more tense and frustrated she became, and of course, her mare responded with even more tension and misbehavior. The more Lucy acted up, the harsher Michaela became with her self-criticism. The tension would often build until Michaela left the lesson in tears. Her NST ran the show, and because she believed what it said, its predictions came true.

jump, leading to even more criticism. "See, I *am* a terrible rider!" This becomes a classic self-fulfilling prophecy.

Negative Feedback Loops: The Downward Spiral

NST also triggers self-defeating emotions. If you see yourself as the worm at the bottom of the manure pile, you will probably experience shame. Shame is the most paralyzing emotion there is: it makes you feel worthless and helpless, and it makes you want to crawl under a rock and hide. This makes you less likely to get out there in the saddle, which leads to less effective riding when you do get out there, which makes you feel more like a worm, which makes you want to crawl under a rock and hide—and you're stuck in a miserable NST feedback loop instead of enjoying your riding. Constant criticism is absolutely toxic to confidence, whether it comes from others or from within yourself.

There is a neurological aspect to these NST feedback loops as well. When you think something, that thought travels along neural pathways in the brain and then throughout the body. The more you repeat a particular thought and use that particular neural pathway, the thicker the pathway becomes and the more connections it grows with other neural pathways. Repetitive thoughts and actions thus become like neural grooves or ruts in your brain. If you've ever driven on a dirt road in New England in March, you know how hard it is not to get sucked into the ruts that form in the mud—your tires naturally slide into the ruts. In your brain, your thoughts and behaviors also follow the "ruts" your neurons have created. This is exactly how you form good habits through practice, but it's also how you get stuck in NST loops: the more you use them, the easier it is to get sucked into them.

Negative Attributions: A No-Win Situation

Even after all of this, NST isn't finished wreaking havoc yet! NST causes more trouble by influencing your attributions. Attributions define who and what gets credit for your successes and failures. NST convinces people to attribute their successes to something external (luck, the mood of their horse), and their failures to internal flaws (lack of talent, poor work ethic, general worminess). It blocks out any evidence to the contrary and interprets every event through the lenses of these attributions.

A negative attribution style also views mistakes or problems as *global* and *permanent*, and successes or strengths as *specific* and *temporary*.

Thus, forgetting a movement in a dressage test means, "I stink at memorizing tests," but a correctly ridden test is dismissed as, "Well, at least I got one right." This NST creates a no-win situation. If mistakes mean "I stink," then you'll always stink because mistakes are inevitable! If success only counts for that moment, you'll never develop confidence

JULIE'S STORY: **DIVINE INTERVENTION?**

Our farm has an indoor arena with a fabric roof, and when snow slides off the roof it sounds like a giant zipper. Julie was having a lesson after a big snowstorm and her mare did not appreciate the sound. Every time the snow slid, the mare leaped and twisted and bucked in an outstanding imitation of a rodeo bronco. Julie sat tight and stayed in the saddle the whole time. When I congratulated her on this, she replied, "It was an act of God that I didn't get bucked off!" I laughed and said that with all due respect, I didn't think God had much to do with it.

Julie was attributing her success to something outside of her control. I asked her instead what *she* had done to stay on. It took some hard thinking before she identified factors such as sitting tall and wrapping her legs around her horse. Once she did, though, this gave her a boost of confidence. She changed her negative attribution to the more realistic, "I've developed a good seat and leg so I can stay in the saddle when my horse acts up."

Remembering this incident later as a result of her own skill rather than divine intervention, she felt more confident the next time the snow slid off the roof, and she could just laugh at her horse's antics. Not surprisingly, her confidence also made her horse calm down a lot more quickly than she had in the previous snowstorm. As Julie learned to attribute her successes to her skills as a rider, she became more willing to try new things, such as going trail riding alone.

and trust in your abilities; in the next moment you could make a mistake, and then your NST will say, "See? I told you that you stink." And since NST sees anything positive as temporary and a result of luck or outside forces, any good experience feels like just a lucky break in between the bad ones. Holding on to a negative attribution style is a guaranteed way to feel incompetent pretty much all of the time.

Watch Your Language!

So how do you escape this loop of NST and terrible feelings? The first step is what our moms taught us: watch your language and be polite! You wouldn't talk to your friends this way, so why are you being so mean and nasty to yourself? You don't deserve to be mistreated by anyone, including you. Any time you hear your NST say something mean and critical, remind it to be polite and encouraging. For example, change "You'll never get this right" to "You're really having trouble with this now, but you can get it if you stick with it."

This doesn't sugarcoat the problem, but it changes the tone from harsh criticism to compassionate encouragement. If that feels too easy-going for you, you can be tough on yourself without being mean or nasty: "Come on, I know you can do better than that, show me what you've got!" This will give you much more motivation and confidence than, "You stink, that's just pathetic."

POSITIVE SELF-TALK: THESE AREN'T YOUR GRANDMOTHER'S "AFFIRMATIONS"

Once you're being more polite and encouraging to yourself, it's time to change NST to PST—Positive Self-Talk. Many people groan and roll their eyes when I bring this up. "I've tried this positive affirmation stuff and it doesn't work. Telling myself 'I'm a great rider' just feels fake." Actually, I agree with this wholeheartedly. You can tell yourself "I'm a wonderful rider" a thousand times, but the committee in your head is just going to shout, "LIAR!" without something more solid to back up that statement. "Affirmations" often fail because they are vague and have no evidence in the real world to support them. The Lizard Brain knows this and rejects them. PST, on the other hand, is based on evidence and is realistic.

Be aware of your attributions and change them when NST creeps in. If you do a canter transition well, note what you did right. "I'm really

MICHELLE AND TERRY'S STORY:
IT WAS A BAD DAY…OR WAS IT?

Michelle crosses the finish line of the cross-country course with a scowl on her face. "It was terrible. We stopped at the water because I didn't have enough leg on. I'm such an idiot."

Terry, on the other hand, finishes with a smile. "I'm bummed because I forgot to put my leg on at the water and he stopped. I got him to go through it on the second try though, and we jumped the rest of the course really well!"

Both riders had the same problem, but Michelle returns to the barn feeling discouraged while Terry feels happy and confident. Michelle is focused exclusively on what went wrong, and she attributes this to permanent qualities within herself ("idiot"). She is unable to see that much of the course went well and that she solved a problem successfully. Terry's PST is not fake or unrealistic; she acknowledges the problem that needs work, but also the many positives that occurred. She takes responsibility for the successes *and* the failures, not just the failures. She feels more confident and has a more realistic view of her abilities as a result.

getting better at staying with my horse's motion." When you make a mistake, describe the problem in specific rather than global terms: "I tensed up that time. I need to sit up and relax my seat." Notice the whole picture, not just the problem: "I got off balance when my horse spooked, but I stayed on this time—I used to fall off when he did that."

When NST is an old habit, it may be stubbornly resistant to giving up its space in your brain. It may reject your attempts at PST with comments like "Nice try with that positive crap, but you and I both know it's not true. You're still a lousy rider." If your brain keeps rejecting your attempts at PST, frame your PST statements as possibilities. Use words like "maybe" or "might," or phrases such as "I am working toward...." These are harder for NST to attack. Some PST statements like this could be:

• "I got almost all of my canter transitions right. Maybe I'm really learning to ride them better."

• "I am working toward being quieter with my hands. Today was better than yesterday."

Positive Events

Do you have difficulty keeping positive events in your mind? Write them down. After every ride, note down at least three things that you did well—*not perfectly*, just well! If you can't think of three things you did well, write down three things that weren't bad.

If that doesn't work, write down three things that could have been a lot worse! It takes practice to notice the positive, and everyone has truly awful days, but PST helps you to find the value in even the most difficult situations. Writing it down makes it more real.

If you hate journals, text the list to yourself or use a smartphone app to keep the list. Glance at it occasionally so that, in Julie's words, "I have some proof that I don't stink."

PST is not an attempt to turn yourself into Susie Sunshine or to ignore problems when they occur. Instead, it helps you to have a realistically positive outlook and builds confidence in your strengths and ability to solve problems, which in turn leads to better riding—and more enjoyment in the whole experience.

Exercise: Turn It Around: Practice Changing NST into PST

On a piece of paper or in your journal, make two columns. Write down three negative things you often say to yourself in the left hand column. In the right hand column, write something positive you can say instead. Remember that Positive Self-Talk (PST) should be encouraging, realistic, and give you credit for both your successes and your mistakes. Remember my Negative Self-Talk (NST) at the beginning of the chapter? "Everyone else here is better than you. You have no business being here. What made you think you could compete against these pros when you're just a hack?" My PST statement could be, "There are a lot of riders here with a lot more experience, but they were all in my shoes at one time. I've trained hard for this and I'm as ready as I know how to be. I'm going to watch them and see what else I can learn."

BRAIN TRAPS

Earlier I gave you a layperson's explanation of how habits are formed in the brain: the more you do a certain behavior or thought, the more you "groove" that thought or behavior into your brain so that you slide into it quite automatically (p. 44). This is great when you've practiced following with your seat at the canter for hours on end. However, when you repeat the wrong thing for hours on end, you get really good at doing the wrong thing, such as leaning up the neck over a jump.

This is true for our mental habits as well: we get very good at whatever thoughts we practice the most. There are several particular thought patterns that cause major damage to a rider's confidence. The psychological term for them is "cognitive distortions." I just call them Brain Traps. There are a wide variety of them, but these are the ones I see riders (myself included) fall into the most. See if you can spot yourself in any of them.

Brain Trap 1: Treating Problems as Character Flaws

"I got impatient with my horse today. I'm such a witch." "I can't believe I'm scared of such a little jump. I'm so stupid." People caught in this trap treat their mistakes and weaknesses as a sign that they are horrible human beings (or even worms at the bottom of the manure pile). They end up feeling horribly guilty, embarrassed, or ashamed when they don't perform well.

As I discussed earlier, this trap can suck the life right out of you, because guilt and shame are paralyzing emotions that make you want to run and hide. Moreover, it's simply not true that making mistakes and being imperfect means that you're a terrible person. It just means you're a person.

The Way Out: People Are Not Problems

How do you escape the Character Flaw trap? Instead of making your character the problem, make the problem the problem. Describe the issue in specific, concrete language and frame it as a problem to be solved. Instead of, "I'm a witch because I got impatient," describe the problem: "I had a hard time staying calm when my horse acted up today. I need to learn how to take it less personally when he does that." Now the problem is "learning to take things less personally" instead of, "I'm a witch." Changing a character flaw feels next to impossible, but describing the problem gives you a road map for where to go next. Much more empowering!

Brain Trap 2: "Catastrophizing"

When you "catastrophize," you tell yourself worst-case scenario stories. "My horse will spook and bolt, and I'll fall off, break my neck and die." "He'll refuse the jump, I'll get eliminated and I'll die of embarrassment." If you're caught in the Catastrophe Trap, you can imagine a horrible death in exquisite detail, either by physical or emotional cause. You are sure you will never get over this particular riding problem and you will always feel as horrible about it as you do now. You may also tell yourself stories about being paralyzed or disabled for the rest of your life. People in the Catastrophe Trap often justify it with stories of friends/relatives/acquaintances who have been harmed in such scenarios, or they remind everyone of how actor Christopher Reeve got paralyzed in a riding accident. They see their fear as legitimate because they have proof that IT COULD HAPPEN!

There are a couple of major flaws in this logic. The first is that while people do get seriously hurt or even die riding, it's actually quite a rare occurrence. We just hear about it a lot more often now because we can watch the accident on YouTube even when it took place halfway around the world only five minutes ago. (Although why anyone would do that to themselves, I still don't understand.)

The second mistake that "catastrophizers" make is to believe that risk is an all-or-nothing proposition: either you're perfectly safe or you're dead. The reality, though, is that you're taking a calculated risk when you ride: it can be dangerous (as many things in life can be), but you've taken appropriate steps to minimize the risk by developing your riding skills.

The biggest problem with "catastrophizing" goes back to the Fight or Flight Response (FOFR) in chapter 2 (p. 25). Remember how I said that the brain can't tell the difference between a real threat and an imagined one? This is where that fact plays out. When you imagine the worst-case scenario—especially one that ends in the brain's primary fear, death—the brain believes it's true and kicks into full Fight or

Flight mode. You've just triggered a tremendous attack of anxiety about something that has not happened.

Now you have a huge surge of adrenaline kicking around in your bloodstream with no saber-toothed tiger around to fight so you can burn it off. This feels awful, and it also makes you less effective in a stressful situation—your body tenses up and your logical thinking shuts off when the FOFR is activated, remember? Some people claim that "catastrophizing" helps prepare them in case something terrible happens, but it actually just makes them even more tense in the moment and saps them of their problem-solving abilities.

The Way Out: Tell Better Stories

How do you extract yourself from the Catastrophe Trap? It's a three-step process. First, accept that there are things in the world that are beyond your control, and make a decision to give up worrying about them (repeat as often as necessary; you may have to do it hundreds of times at the beginning).

Second, tell yourself different stories. Instead of telling yourself the worst-case scenario, tell yourself what a likely scenario would be. Take the spook/bolt/break neck/die scenario and ask yourself, "What is most likely to happen?" The answer might be something like "My horse might spook and spin, but he's done that before and I've learned to recognize that it's coming so I can stay on." Or you can go back to the reassurance step in chapter 3: "I will probably get over the jump on the second try even if he stops the first time. And even if I get eliminated, I would hate it but I could live with it." Notice that again, we're not trying to make things all sunshiny and perfect, just realistic.

The third step is to notice when you're wrong and appreciate it. "Hey, he didn't spook at all and we had a great ride!" You can pry yourself right out of the Catastrophe Trap when you pay attention to all of the times that things go just fine. Make a habit out of noticing when things go well.

Brain Trap 3: Giving Anxiety Too Much Airtime

I've had many students over the years who have walked into the ring and told me that they're really nervous on that particular day. This isn't a problem in and of itself, but it becomes a trap if the anxiety becomes the focus, because what you focus on gets bigger. Have you ever noticed that someone has food on her face, and suddenly you can't even hear what she's saying because you're so distracted by the food? When anxiety is given the floor for too long, the same thing happens—you can't think of anything else.

Riders who are caught in the Airtime Trap usually believe that they have to get rid of their fears before they can do anything challenging, so they think they have to talk about them until they don't feel them anymore. This is a great idea, except that it almost never works. The more airtime the fear gets, the more scary stories it can come up with, and the more the FOFR is activated. The next thing we know, the rider is on a fast train to Panicville and the fear has hijacked the entire ride.

The Way Out: Pay Attention to What You *Can* Do

To get yourself out of the Airtime Trap, focus on your skills. Use the Plan in chapter 3 to answer your fear's "What if?" so that your brain knows you have the skills to solve whatever problem might arise (p. 33). If you aren't sure you do have those skills, talk to your trainer or another knowledgeable person about what you should do to solve a particular problem, instead of just talking about how nervous you are. If you need to air your anxiety to relieve some stress, make sure you also talk about what you are going to do to address it. When your fear has a plan, it can step back and let you get on with the business of riding.

People caught in the Airtime Trap often have difficulty shifting their focus at first; their brains want to pull them back into "What if?" If your worries keep stepping in front of you, keep reminding them of your plan and ask them to step aside. Remember that it helps to treat your worries as entities that are separate from you, so talk to them directly: "I appreciate your looking out for me, but I've got it covered. I'm going to ride now." One rider I teach just says "Stop" when her worries start nattering at her. Be as firm as you need to, as often as you need to. Like everything else, it gets easier with practice.

Brain Trap 4: Telling War Stories

- "I had a huge crash over that jump a few years ago."

- "You should have seen how hard my horse bucked!"

- "Did you see the video of that rider's rotational fall? The horse's neck...."

I won't go on, because my amygdala is pretty sure it needs to call out the adrenaline troops right now, and I can't write coherently when my Lizard Brain is running the show. We humans have a strange need to talk about our scary and painful experiences. This explains "thrills-and-spills" videos and women's conversations about the agonies of child-birth. Sometimes it makes things less scary to talk about them, but at other times, it backfires. If you're struggling with your confidence, avoid the War Stories Trap like a saber-toothed tiger.

Again, the brain doesn't know the difference between real and imagined, so when you call up a scary memory, all the emotions associated with that memory come flooding in with it. If it's someone else's experience, your Lizard Brain pictures the scenario and reacts as if it's happening to you. When you're working to improve your confidence, the last thing you need is for your FOFR to get triggered when there's no real danger around.

The Way Out: Change the Subject

Avoiding the War Stories Trap is pretty simple: don't tell such stories, and don't listen to them. Stay away from those "thrills-and-spills" videos and anything else posted online that shows people falling and getting hurt. If a group of people are going on about their scariest moments, excuse yourself from the conversation or change the subject. You can often be quite direct with other riders and say something like, "Hey, I'm really trying to become more confident, and this conversation is freaking me out. Can we talk about something else?"

If non-riders want to know about your dangerous moments, say that you don't like to talk about them. It's not rude, it's self-protective, and most people will respect that. Lots of people who witnessed my fall a few years ago have asked me about it, and I tell them that I don't really want to talk about it, since I'm over it and I'm not scared and don't want to become so. No one has ever pushed me on it.

Please note, I am not saying that you should never talk about your scary experiences. I *am* a therapist after all, and I believe very strongly in the power of talking about pain in order to heal. However, this is not usually what happens in the War Stories Trap. If you need to talk about a painful experience, find a supportive listener rather than a group situation where you're at risk for becoming retraumatized.

Brain Trap 5: Remembering the Fear, But Not the Success

At our barn this is also known as "I almost died!" "But you didn't." "But I *could have!*" We all have near-misses in riding; it's part of the unpredictability of sitting on a 1000-pound flight animal. But they're *near* misses, not misses, and it's important to remember that. We got out of them. Or, even if they were actual misses, we're still here.

Riders in this Near-Miss Trap get stuck on the scary part of the situation and forget that they handled it successfully. Because they can't see their positive actions, they can't get past the fear.

The Way Out: Notice How the Story Ends

The way out of this Near Miss Trap is to change your language from "I

MY STORY: **SPRING HACK**

I was hacking with a mother and her daughter out on a back road one spring, and the daughter's pony bolted for home. Of course, the mother's horse took off in hot pursuit. I couldn't catch them and they ran all the way back to the barn.

The child was fine; Mom, not so much. With a true *negative attribution* style, she was convinced that she'd only stayed on her horse out of pure luck (interestingly, she was sure her daughter had done a fabulous job of staying calm and remembering what to do). I acknowledged that the situation had been a scary one, but that she and her daughter had both kept their balance and maintained a safe position on the side of the road (even if the brakes didn't work), and everything had worked out.

almost died!" to "Wow, that was scary, but I got through it!" You need to notice what you did correctly to help the situation, and notice that things often start badly but end just fine. If you did have a fall and possibly got hurt, notice that you really didn't die (your Lizard Brain needs you to point this out!) and that you're brave enough to come back and try again. Notice the success, and give yourself credit for having some role in that success.

Remember that you always have a choice about where to focus your attention, and when you give something your attention, you give it power. By giving your attention to your success in handling a difficult situation, you will feel more confident the next time you're in a jam.

Brain Trap 6: Overgeneralizing

I own a chestnut Thoroughbred mare. What image just popped into your head? A wild child with rolling eyes and flaring nostrils that is on the verge of bolting? If so, you've fallen into the Overgeneralizing Trap when it comes to redheaded TB girls. It turns out that she's incredibly lazy and has the personality of a golden retriever: she'd rather nap in your lap than run across a field. However, any time she does act up, someone always shakes her head and says, "Well, she's a chestnut mare all right."

The Overgeneralizing Trap kicks in when you experience something and assume that this is always the case: chestnut mares are wild, ponies are naughty, riders from Australia are crazy. (Although I do think that last one might be true!)

In the case of Brain Traps, you experience a problem and then assume that it will continue to occur. I see this happen a lot with riders of young horses: their horse takes a little while to walk into a stream on a trail, and I later hear them say, "My horse doesn't like water." Or a rider has a fall while jumping an oxer and she thinks, "I'm no good at oxers."

Overgeneralizing is a problem because it creates a self-fulfilling prophecy: you assume your horse hates water, so you're anxious when you approach the water. You unwittingly take your leg off because you're anxious, and your horse stops. "See? I told you he doesn't like water."

Once again, this tendency evolved for a good reason: to protect us from threats. Our ancestors couldn't afford to wait around and see whether this was a poisonous snake or a wavy stick on the ground; they just reacted to "squiggly object on the ground" with "Snake! Run away!" However, it becomes detrimental when you see a problem and assume you will have that problem all the time, in every situation. (One workshop participant called this a "terminal problem"—she worried that it would be there until she died!)

The Way Out: Stick to Specifics; Envision a Different Future

There are two simple ways out of the Overgeneralizing Trap. The first is to describe a problem in very specific terms. "My horse stopped at the water a couple of times today. We did eventually get him to go in." "I had a fall at an oxer last week, so I'm nervous right now about jumping an oxer again." Keeping it specific—*this* thing happened at *this* time, and I'm feeling *this way* about it *right now*—makes it much easier to come up with a plan and a solution, and it makes it less contagious to other situations.

The second strategy is to describe a problem in the past tense, and then describe a solution in the present or future tense. "We have had some trouble with water before, but we're going to improve that today." "I was lacking confidence over oxers, but I'm practicing them so I can feel better about them." This allows your brain to envision a future that's different from the past, rather than assuming that the problem is always true. The brain is extremely sensitive to language, so be sure you use your words effectively!

Brain Trap 7: Judging Your Insides by Other People's Outsides

Students often tell me I can't possibly understand their anxiety about cross-country jumping because, "You're so brave, you just go and jump the big stuff like it's no big deal." They're comparing their *insides,* which are a bundle of nerves, to my *outside* persona, which looks calm and focused (more on that in a later chapter). They have no idea that beneath that exterior is often a churning mess! They are also looking only at the end result, and not the hours upon hours of practice and problem solving that I do every day of every week. When they get to a show, they think they're the only person who is nervous because they don't see terror on anyone's face. In reality, those faces are hiding a multitude of emotions!

The Inside/Outside Trap makes you feel like you're the only person in the world with a particular feeling or problem. This leaves you feeling isolated and discouraged, when the truth is that nearly every rider has the same feelings and problems at one time or another. You just happen to know what's beneath your own mask, while you can't see through the masks that others are wearing.

Another version of the Inside/Outside Trap is the thought that "so-and-so has it easy because she has more money/nicer horses/more supportive family members/more connections," and so on. This is a nice comfy trap for many people because it lets them make excuses for why they aren't further along with their own goals: "If I had her bank account, obviously I'd be doing the High Amateur Jumpers by now." "Of course she's a better rider. She doesn't have kids so she can focus totally on her horses."

This trap is especially seductive because it's usually partly true: more money, nicer horses, a kid-free existence do make it easier to become better. But it also discounts the very real hard work that the more "privileged" person is doing. Every good rider I know from every tax bracket has to work extremely hard to be as good as they are, and they all run into difficulties with their horses and their riding skills. Truly outstanding riders don't waste their time worrying about whether someone else has it better than they do; they figure out what they have to do to get better, and then they go and do it again and again.

The Way Out: Separate Fact From Fiction

In order to escape from the Inside/Outside Trap, you need to recognize that you are making up stories about the people around you. You must realize that you can't read anyone's mind; you can't tell just by looking at them what they are thinking and how they are feeling. Once you recognize you're trapped, you can simply ignore your stories, or you can tell yourself different stories that make you feel better. In this case, it doesn't matter if they're true; it only matters if they're useful. (You're creating fiction either way; you might as well create stories that make you feel better!)

So, if you think that the woman doing her test just before you is perfectly calm, cool and collected, imagine her working hard to control her nerves as she rides. Imagine that the Big Name Rider walking his course in front of you is seriously worried about how his young horse is going to handle the Novice water crossing (this is almost always true). If you feel envious because things seem to come more easily to someone else, think of people you know who have come from the bottom and have worked their way to the top.

Changing your stories not only makes you feel better, it often makes you more empathetic toward other riders, which lessens your feelings of isolation.

Another escape route out of the Inside/Outside Trap is to spend time talking to riders who have more experience than you do. Ask them whether they have the same feelings that you do, and how they handle them. Don't be shy about this; most riders are happy to share their experiences, especially in more relaxed situations such as in the tack room or at the wine and cheese party at the end of the show day.

I have asked a lot of riders I admire about their inner experiences and I've found they go through all of the same emotions that I do, just

MY STORY: **WE'VE ALL BEEN THERE**

Some years ago I was struggling with a lot of frustration and impatience with the first horse I ever trained, and I was sure I was the most horrible trainer in the world for feeling that way. At a clinic I attended, the clinician (an Olympic medalist) was talking about the importance of patience in the training process. Feeling like a worm, I asked him if it was harder for him to maintain this with his own horses versus the horses he rode for other owners. "Of course it's harder. You always have more invested when it's your own," he responded. I felt a huge wave of relief wash over me. If an Olympic rider got impatient sometimes, it meant I wasn't horrible, I just needed to learn more tools to cope with my case of "own-horse syndrome"!

at a higher level. This helps me feel less intimidated by better riders, which allows me to shift my focus toward improving my own riding.

Brain Trap 8: Minimizing Abilities and Exaggerating Weaknesses

I touched on this Minimize/Exaggerate Trap in the section about Owning your Abilities in chapter 2 (p. 36). We tend to fall into this trap out of habit, because it's a social convention. How did you respond the last time someone gave you a compliment, about your riding or about anything else? If you're like a lot of people you probably either gave a compliment back or you put yourself down in some way. Here's how this conversation often goes:

Person 1: "Wow, you rode beautifully in that class!"

Person 2: "Oh, I was a hot mess! I picked up the wrong lead in my lope, right in front of the judge."

Person 1: "You fixed it so fast I bet he barely even saw it. You always look so poised. I wish my position was as nice as yours!"

Person 2: "Are you kidding? You can ride circles around me! I've never even seen your horse get too quick in the lope, never mind pick up the wrong lead."

In social terms, everyone in this conversation played their role correctly. Person 1 made Person 2 feel good, but Person 2 discounted the compliment in order to appear modest. Person 1 then repeated the compliment while downplaying her own abilities, and Person 2 complimented Person 1. While this may satisfy social convention, it's terrible for the confidence of both people. Remember, the more you are criticized by yourself or others, the more likely you are to believe the criticism. Conversely, you have to own your abilities in order to feel confident about them. This interaction undermines you instead of making you more sure of yourself.

MY STORY: **HOW TO ACCEPT A COMPLIMENT**

My husband taught me how to escape from this trap. When we were dating he would compliment me on something, and being a typical American woman, I would discount the remark in one way or another. Apparently one day he'd had enough, because he got really angry at me. "You make me feel stupid when you do that!" he shouted (and he *never* shouts). "For once in your life, say thank you and *shut up!*" Stunned, I mumbled a meek, "Thank you." Then something interesting happened: over the course of the next few weeks, when I got a compliment, I said, "Thank you," and then, well, I shut up. It felt awkward at first, but then I started to really *hear* the compliment. It slowly dawned on me that maybe the people really meant the compliment, and maybe they saw something in me that I didn't see. Gradually those compliments started to feel really good, and I was eventually able to see in myself what the other person saw in me.

This was truly life-changing for me. So the next time you're given a compliment, resist the temptation to discount or downplay it; say thank you and then just stop talking! You will be amazed at how reflexive it is to deflect positive feedback from others, but you will eventually start to hear it and take it in. I told this story to a group of adults at a weeklong riding camp, and they entertained themselves for the rest of the week telling each other, "Say thank you—now shut up," after the instructor said something positive!

Brain Trap 9: Perfectionism

In reasonable doses, perfectionism is a great asset for riders: it keeps you striving to learn and improve and never lets you settle for less than 100 percent. It becomes a trap, though, if you are only happy with yourself and your horse when the ride is perfect. Perfection is unattainable in living beings because they change and move from moment to moment: balance is gained then lost, movement is beautiful then a wobbling step is taken, the arc over a jump is breathtaking then there is a stumble upon landing. Perfection also implies that something is finished, and riding is not something that is ever complete. There is always more to learn, more strength to build, more harmony to achieve between you and your horse.

If you can only be happy with perfection, you'll be miserable most of the time. Perfection happens in moments, not as an end result. It's also unfair to expect perfection from our horses. Let's face it, if left to their own devices, they would never piaffe or jog or jump a triple combination—they'd hang out eating grass and occasionally chase each other around for fun! It's amazing that they try so hard for us at all; we owe it to them to give them room to make mistakes. Of all of the brain traps, I think the Perfectionism Trap offers the quickest and most direct path to unhappiness, frustration, and discouragement.

The Way Out: Be Excellent!

If you're caught in the Perfectionism Trap, you obviously care very deeply about your riding, and this is a good thing. I'm not going to tell you to "settle" for anything or not to care about your mistakes. Instead, think of *excellence* as your goal rather than *perfection*. Excellence is a challenge, but an ongoing, achievable challenge, instead of a fixed, unattainable one.

Aiming for excellence means recognizing all of the small steps of progress and not just the completed goal. Maybe your horse hasn't mastered his flying changes, but he's starting to understand what you're asking for. Get excited about that! He can't do his changes until he's figured out what you want, so you might as well celebrate the achievement of that step along the way!

When you celebrate progress instead of waiting until everything is "perfect" to enjoy it, your rides become a lot more fun and a lot more rewarding on a daily basis. You will also be kinder to your horse, because you will know when to call it a day instead of insisting that he does something "one more time" in an attempt to get it right.

Here are two ways to focus on excellence rather than perfection. The first comes from the segment in chapter 2 about recognizing your strengths: Every day, note three things that you did well, or that you did better than you did the day before (p. 37). Avoid any "yes but" talk, just list the three things.

The second strategy is to rate things on a scale of zero to "10." Your canter transition wasn't "okay," it was a "6." Your distance wasn't "pretty good," it was an "8." That halt wasn't "horrible," it was a "3." This helps you develop a sense of perspective instead of going into the all-or-nothing mindset of perfectionism.

 ## Exercise: Escape From Your Brain Traps

List the most common Brain Trap(s) that you tend to fall into, then write out what you can do when you see that you're starting to slip into them.

RESTRUCTURING THE COMMITTEE

I mentioned earlier that many of us have a "committee" in our heads that keeps a running commentary on everything that we do. This committee is mostly negative and sometimes downright vicious. It's often made up of voices from our past: a parent, a harsh instructor, a nasty schoolmate. If your committee is making you feel like a horrible rider (or a horrible person), it's time for some organizational restructuring—in other words, fire them.

This often takes some serious work, and if your committee is wreaking havoc in your life in general, you may want to enlist the help of a therapist or other supportive person. Many of these voices have lived inside your head for years, if not your entire life, and they are unlikely to go quietly. Having a supportive friend or counselor to lean on can give you a shot of courage when the Committee tries to shout you down.

Clear Out the Current Members

The first step to firing negative or outdated Committee members is simply to notice that you have negative thoughts going through your head—that's your committee weighing in. Now decide that you will not choose to agree with them this time. It turns out that you don't have to believe everything you think! Next, tell them that their services are no longer necessary. The conversation can go like this:

Committee: "You really are a pathetic rider. You've been taking lessons for years and you still can't sit the trot."

Self: "Actually my sitting trot is much better than it used to be. And by the way, I don't want you on my committee anymore. You need to leave now."

Committee: "Are you kidding? We're just telling you the truth."

Self: "No, you're not. You need to leave. You're fired."

Committee: "You can't do that. This position is a lifetime appointment."

Self: "Not anymore, it's not. It's my brain; I get to decide who stays. There's the door. Here, I've packed up all of your things."

This may take many, many repetitions; that's fine, just keep at it. Like everything else, the more you practice this, the easier it gets.

Assemble a Better Committee

Next, it's time to assemble a new committee. This one should be comprised of people who support and encourage you. You might want some of them to be tough on you, and that's okay; just make sure they don't make you feel small or worthless in the process. The committee can be one person or three or five, and the members can be real or imaginary. They might include your favorite character in a novel and your current trainer. For example, one little boy I worked with chose Luke Skywalker to be on his committee; he imagined Luke giving him advice and cheering him on. Whoever the members are, when you are struggling, imagine what they would say to encourage and support you. If they are real people in your life, ask them for support and hear what they have to say. If one member is your favorite author, read her work often for inspiration. Imagine what your favorite character would say if he or she were standing in front of you. Your committee should always have your best interests at heart above everything else.

PRACTICE ANYTIME, ANYWHERE!

Learning to use PST is challenging because so much of our thinking is automatic. However, unlike many other riding skills, you can practice it everywhere, all the time. Catch yourself when you make a negative attribution or fall into a Brain Trap, and redirect your self-talk in more positive directions. With practice, you will find yourself becoming more objective about yourself as a rider, which will help you to improve much more quickly and feel much more confident about your skills. And you may notice a positive trickle-down effect in the rest of your life as well!

PART II

Focus, Confidence, and StressLess Performance

The Keys to Your Brain:
Stressing Less in the Saddle

FOCUSED CALM

"Ride the horse you have now,
not the horse you had two seconds ago."
—Olympic Gold Medalist David O'Connor

So you've met your Inner Lizard, and you've learned to soothe it with reassurance and a plan. You're beginning to catch your Negative Self-Talk and send it in a more positive direction. You're falling less often into your old brain traps. Now it's time to get in the saddle and ride confidently and competently. What do skilled, confident riders do to produce their best performance, at home or in competition?

Think of riders at the top of horse sports: Margie Engle in showjumping, Stacy Westfall in reining, William Fox-Pitt in eventing, Charlotte Dujardin in dressage. Now think of top athletes in other sports: David Ortiz in baseball, Serena Williams in tennis, Tiger Woods in golf. What do they have in common? Talent, obviously. An intense, passionate work ethic. Great coaching. Years of practice, of course. But there is one skill they possess that I believe sets them above all the others, and that skill is *Focus*.

Focus is the ability to stay present in the moment and concentrate completely on the task at hand, to the exclusion of everything else. The focused athlete is able to respond instantly to any situation because he is completely attuned to the present moment; he isn't wondering what might happen, and he isn't distracted by the outside environment or his internal dialogue.

I saw an incredible example of this at the Rolex Kentucky Three Day Event in 2009, at the infamous Head of the Lake water complex. Riders had to jump down a six-foot bank into the water, and then gallop five strides to the right to jump a massive jump made of brush in the middle of the lake. No circling was allowed between the two jumps.

Veteran Olympian Bruce Davidson came into the complex at full speed. His mare jumped boldly down the bank, and seemed to be perfectly lined up with the brush jump in the water, but then she drifted left in mid-air; she clearly wasn't going to make the right hand bend to the brush. Most riders would have had to circle, incurring an unwanted 20 penalty points. Not Bruce: lightning-fast, he made a crazy, but totally legal, left-then-right zigzag back to the brush, jumped it from almost a standstill, and galloped away as though nothing untoward had happened. *And his face never flinched.* (Watch it at https://www.youtube.com/watch?v=3yiT-uKucZ4 or look up "Bruce Davidson Jam Rolex 2009." It's truly amazing.)

After I picked up my jaw from the ground where it had dropped, I realized that what I had just seen was a perfect state of Focused Calm. Bruce wasn't distracted by panic or frustration that his original plan hadn't worked, and he wasn't worrying about whether he might fall off. Focused Calm allowed Bruce to attend to the present moment, and to respond instantly and effectively to what was happening. I realized that day that Focused Calm is the mind/body state that I want to achieve in my riding.

As I said in the Introduction, I have always struggled with sport psychology advice that insists that I need to be relaxed to perform at my best. Relaxation is a feeling I have when I'm having dinner with friends; it's not what I experience when I'm riding my dressage test or navigating a difficult show-jumping course. It's definitely not how I feel when I'm sitting on a green horse who is thinking about going on a bucking spree, either! Focused Calm makes much more sense to me as an ideal performance state: alert, present in the moment, with a supple body that is free of anticipatory tension. The *knowledge* of the Rational Brain and the *adrenaline* of the Lizard Brain are working in harmony instead of at cross-purposes.

Fortunately for those of us who aren't Serena Williams, there is great news about Focused Calm: *Focused Calm is a behavior, not an emotion, a talent, or a personality trait. This means that it can be learned and practiced just like any other riding skill.*

The next time you are watching your favorite rider or other athletes you admire, really stare at them. Notice the facial expression, the body posture, the fluidity of movement. These are deliberately chosen behaviors. Quarterback Peyton Manning gets frustrated when he over-throws the football. Dressage master Isabella Werth is disappointed when she misses a flying change. Serena Williams gets annoyed when she misses a shot. But these athletes maintain the behavior of Focused Calm *regardless of how they are feeling at any given moment.*

As riders, we can do the same. We can stay present in the moment with a supple body and let go of distractions such as our irritation about a mistake or a flapping plastic bag next to the arena. In competition, we can maintain our Focused Calm while feeling our intensity and passion. This creates an ideal performance state, where all of our best traits and skills work together to let us shine.

Focused Calm is simple, but it's challenging to do, and it requires the same repetitive practice as our other riding skills. It might be tempting to go right out and try this at the next show or at the spot where your horse spooked, spun, and left you on the ground. You will get better results, however, if you start with a much less stressful environment, where your Lizard Brain is less likely to be on full alert. You can begin with the following two exercises: the first one developing the Calm, and the second one creating the Focus.

 ## Exercise: The Picture of Focused Calm

This exercise is quite simple: you are going to place your body in a posture of Focused Calm. If you have any photographs of yourself in a state of Focused Calm, riding or otherwise, look at them before you get started so you have a helpful image in your mind.

1 Sit on your horse in a quiet, comfortable environment. Pick up the reins, sit tall, and allow your arms to hang naturally in their neutral position. Place your feet in the stirrups. Let your muscles stay supple. Put a calm expression on your face: smooth your forehead, soften your jaw muscles, let your lips close gently together. Scan your body for any stiffness or tension, and let any tense muscles soften until they feel supple again. You'll know when you have Focused Calm, because it will feel easy and natural, not forced.

2 Next, ask your horse to walk on, and keep your body in its posture of Focused Calm, moving now with the motion of the horse. When this feels easy, do some trot and canter as well. It doesn't matter if you do any real "work" with your horse at this point; the goal is simply to maintain your Focused Calm in all three gaits. Every few strides, check in with your body and make sure you are still riding with a calm expression, supple muscles, and your full attention on the movement of your horse.

3 Now you're going to practice regaining the Focused Calm posture. Walk your horse around, and imagine that he spooks. Tense up your body, lean forward, and do anything else that you tend to do when you're in a stressful situation—scrunch up your facial muscles, breathe faster, whatever. Then take a big breath, breathe it out "soup-breath" style (p. 27), and put yourself back into your Focused Calm position.

4 Do this repeatedly so that your body learns how it feels to go from tense to calm. Practice this at the trot and the canter as well, until you are really familiar with what Focused Calm looks and feels like for you. You may want a friend to take some pictures or video while you're doing this, so that you have a visual image of what you want to achieve.

Now you're going to work on the Focus part of the equation.

 ## Exercise: Single-Point Focus

1 Choose a place to ride where you and your horse are comfortable. First, at the walk, develop a Calm posture in your body: hips supple, elbows soft, shoulder blades back and down.

2 Now focus all of your attention on the sensation of holding the reins in your fingers. Be aware of each finger, of the amount of pressure you place on each rein, of the texture of the reins in your hands.

3 For one full minute, notice only your hands on the reins. Every time your attention wanders to something else in the environment or in your mind, bring it back to the reins in your fingers. This will happen a *lot* in the beginning, so be patient, and just keep bringing your attention back to your hands. Just becoming aware that your mind has wandered is half the battle.

4 Do this at the trot and the canter as well.

5 Practice this daily for 2–4 minutes at a time, choosing one part of your body to focus on—your seat, your shoulders, your feet in the stirrups.

This exercise is much more difficult to do with horses than it is with, say, a tennis racket. As riders, we have to respond constantly to our horse's behavior and adjust accordingly. This can seriously disrupt focus, and you will find yourself repeatedly having to bring your attention back to the original task at hand.

Don't worry about it, and don't give yourself a hard time about it; that's simply the nature of riding. The important thing is to catch your wandering attention and steer it back in the direction that you have chosen. Judging yourself for wandering—"There I go again, I've gotten

MY STORY: **SINGLE-POINT FOCUS…**
OR NOT SO MUCH

I was recently schooling dressage and working on keeping my toes forward as they like to creep into their 45-degree-angle jumping position when I'm not paying attention. I thought I was doing a great job of single-point focus. Actually, though, here's what the inside of my head sounded like:

"There. Toes forward. Good. No, don't pull your leg up, stretch it down. Hmm, he's falling behind my leg. No wonder my position looks so awful in those photos from last summer at Millbrook, if I keep pulling my leg up and letting my toes go out like that. At least he was so relaxed in that test. I wish I could figure out how to keep him that way all the time. When my toe is forward and my legs are down, though, he's less electric. I need to remember to point that out to Carolyn, too, because her horse gets electric to her leg also."

So much for single-point focus! I'd fallen completely out of the moment and into my interior monologue *about* the moment. Once I caught myself, I had to remember not to go on another monologue about my frustration with myself for my lack of focus; instead, I needed to say "toes forward" and get on with it.

distracted. I can't do this focus thing. No wonder I have so much trouble keeping my act together in the ring"—is just another form of wandering. Just notice, refocus. Notice, refocus. Put your body back into a Calm posture each time you bring your attention back.

Be aware, too, of the sneakier form of distraction: the interior mono-logue. It makes you *think* that you're focused, but really, you're not in the moment at all; you're completely caught up in your inner conversation.

As you practice Focused Calm, you will find that you can catch yourself more quickly when your mind wanders. You will also be able to respond more quickly to your horse's behavior. You'll be able to stop a spook or a run-out at a jump because you'll notice quickly what he is doing, rather than being distracted by thoughts of what he *might* do. You'll notice his attention wandering, because you'll see his ear twitch in a different direction. As you improve your attention to the moment, you will find yourself acting calm and effective in more and more chal-lenging situations, and your confidence will grow as a result.

In high-stress situations, it can be much more difficult to do Focused Calm. The Lizard Brain kicks into high gear and tries to grab the reins, while telling you awful stories about what could happen next. You need some extra tools to stay in Focused Calm in those situations.

Real Self and Performance Self: The Two Sides of You

In *The New Toughness Training for Sports,* psychologist Jim Loehr describes two distinct selves that we have within us: our Real Self and our Performance Self. The Real Self is just what it sounds like: the real me, with all of my needs, emotions, worries, dreams, and responsibili-ties. At any given moment, my Real Self may be thinking about the guy who cut me off in traffic on the way to the barn, making a grocery list, getting annoyed because my fingers are cold, or wondering whether I remembered to turn off the heat in the tack room when I left it. My Real Self cares very much whether I do a good job in my lesson, what my trainer thinks of my riding, and whether I'm going to be successful at my next show.

The Performance Self, on the other hand, is the persona you step into when you need to perform at your best. Most of us have one of these in our work lives, at the very least. The Performance Self lives completely in the present moment. It isn't worrying about the guy who cut you off or the heat in the tack room; it leaves those concerns to the Real Self. The Performance Self knows and trusts all of your skills and abilities, and it only cares about the task at hand. It doesn't feel cold, hot, tired, or hungry. It doesn't care about what others think, not even your trainer. It doesn't even care about winning, because winning is the by-product of performance—it's in the future, and the Performance Self only exists in the present. The Performance Self leaves all of those concerns to the Real Self and zeros in on what to do in this moment, right now.

Think of times when you have been 100 percent in Performance Self as a rider. Picture your posture, your facial expression. Better yet, look at a photo of yourself in this state. (I splurge a lot on professional photos of my riding at shows so I can surround myself with images of my Performance Self.) What were you thinking at that moment? What were you feeling? I guarantee you weren't concerned with what your trainer was thinking or if your horse was going to spook at the flowers around the ring. You were 100 percent in the present moment, doing what needed to be done right then.

 ## Exercise: Performance Self

Take a moment to list some qualities that illustrate your performance self. If possible, find a picture of yourself in this state. Describe your:
- Facial Expression
- Muscle Tone
- Body Posture
- Attitude Your Posture Conveys (Calm, Intense, Focused, Happy)

It's Not About the Result—It's About This Moment, Right Now

Dropping out of Performance Self and back into Real Self when you are riding often disrupts your performance. Many top riders tell stories of having the ride of their lives, and then they fall back into Real Self with something like "One more jump, and I've won the championship," and sure enough, they knock a jump down, and lose first place. Conversely, many athletes will say after a big win that they weren't thinking about winning at the time; their focus was on completing the pass, making the putt, riding the final halt perfectly square.

Staying in Performance Self allows you to be completely absorbed in the moment, and thus completely in tune with your horse, able to respond quickly and instinctively to whatever happens. Luckily enough, it allows you to get the most enjoyment out of your rides, as well!

Each time you ride, put on your Performance Self. Set your Real Self aside for later. If your Lizard Brain objects, "HELLO, SELF, WE HAVE REALLY IMPORTANT STUFF TO WORRY ABOUT," reassure it that you will take care of those things after you ride. I use my grooming and tacking-up time to make the transition from Real Self to Performance Self. As I put on my boots, gloves, and helmet, I'm putting on my Performance Self. I tell my Real Self to wait for me in the tack room and assure it that I'll be back in plenty of time to take care of anything it needs. (Corny? Definitely. But I'll do anything if it works.)

Three Strategies for Staying in Performance Self and Maintaining Focused Calm

Say Delete

Getting into Performance Self is one thing, but staying there is another. Outside distractions, strong emotions, and extraneous thoughts try constantly to wedge themselves in, disrupting your Focused Calm and breaking the shell of your Performance Self. Your riding time is *not* the time to stop and analyze those emotions and thoughts, so you need a quick, simple way to get rid of them. My favorite trick is to say the word "Delete."

Now, before you roll your eyes, remember what I said in the Introduction: try it before you decide that it won't work. When I first heard about using, "Delete," I thought it was a corny and ridiculous gimmick—then I tried it. But to my amazement, a few minutes later, I realized I'd let go of the problem thought and was back on task. It's now my automatic response to any distracting thought or image in my mind.

"Delete" works for several reasons. One, it's short, so I can refocus quickly. Two, my brain instantly knows what I mean because I do it dozens of times a day when I send a text or an email. Third, it's a neutral word, so it doesn't trigger another emotion that I would then have to deal with.

If you don't care for "Delete," find another word that shifts your attention; just be sure to keep it short. Short and simple is critical, because if the brain goes into a long analysis/explanation monologue— "There I go again, I'm letting myself get distracted by outside thoughts, I need to turn those off and get back to business"—you have already slipped out of Performance Self and wasted several strides with all of that excess verbiage. "Delete" or another single-word cue lets you immediately return to Performance Self and your state of Focused Calm.

 ### Exercise: "Delete" Extraneous Thoughts

1 Set a timer for two minutes. Now, either in your actual kitchen or in your imagination, make a peanut butter and jelly sandwich. In those two minutes, if any thought enters your mind that is unrelated to the assembling of that sandwich, say "Delete" out loud, then return your attention to the sandwich. Thoughts about needing to go grocery shopping? Delete. Thoughts about why your kids never put their dishes in the dishwasher? Delete. Thoughts that this is the dumbest exercise you've ever done? Delete, Delete, Delete. Refocus on the smell of the bread, the feel of the knife dipping into the jar, the crumbs on the counter.

2 After the two minutes are up, notice how you feel. Do you feel calm and focused? Great. Enjoy your sandwich. Do you feel frustrated that you had to say "Delete" a bazillion times? No problem—just "Delete" your judgment that you shouldn't have to say "Delete" so much, and return your focus to the sandwich.

As you go through your days over the next few weeks, practice deleting distracting thoughts that interfere with what you're doing. It's especially useful in frustrating traffic situations or with negative, self-critical thoughts that make you feel bad about yourself.

When you apply this to your riding, delete any thought that does not contribute to improving this situation *in this moment right now.* That means that if you're approaching the "scary" corner of the arena, delete thoughts such as, "He's going to spook and I'll fall off!" and "He hates this corner." That leaves more room for solution-focused thoughts such as, "I need to keep his attention on me so I'm going to bend him to the inside just before the corner." Deleting unnecessary or confidence-killing thoughts leaves more room in your Rational Brain for problem-solving.

While "Delete" is useful for worries about the future, it's also an excellent strategy for recovering from mistakes and letting go of past negative experiences. When something negative happens, it's very easy to get stuck in that moment and spend a lot of time focusing on how that mistake is going to affect your desired outcome.

For example, when my horse has broken from the canter before I've finished a circle, I've gotten stuck in thoughts like, "I can't believe she just broke. That was such a great canter, but now it's going to get a '4' instead of an '8.'" Meanwhile, I've just lost four strides to those thoughts, when I should have been setting up for the next movement.

The quote from David O'Connor that started this chapter summarizes this perfectly: "Ride the horse you have now, not the horse you had two seconds ago." You can't get those two seconds back. "Delete" the mistake as soon as it happens, and put your Focused Calm behavior back in place so that you can improve the only thing you can control: the present moment.

Two-Beat Mantra

Another strategy for maintaining Focused Calm is the Two-Beat Mantra. This is a phrase that you repeat to yourself, in rhythm with your horse's stride, that reminds you of what you need to do to be effective in a challenging situation. For example, if you are approaching The Evil Mailbox at the neighbor's house and you want to avoid tensing up, your mantra might be, "Breathe and soften, breathe and soften."

If you tend to lean at your jumps, your mantra might be, "Sit tall, sit tall." When I have a lot of generalized panicky Lizard Brain chatter in my head, my mantra is, "Shut up and ride, shut up and ride!"

All mantras are not created equal. A "cheerleader" mantra that's just designed to distract you from your churning emotions and make you feel good—"We're the best, forget the rest" is one I heard somewhere—doesn't help your brain do its job. The phrase needs to cue your brain *to remember what it knows how to do,* so that you can be effective, not distracted. Hollow platitudes are mental clutter at best, and at worst, they will trigger your Lizard Brain's Faker Identification System. You don't need your Lizard Brain shouting, "LIAR! We are NOT the best!" when you're trying to get the job done!

Whatever your mantra is (it will change depending on the situation), it should be only two beats long, so that you won't have to think about several things at once, and you can repeat it in rhythm with your horse's stride. This also helps you maintain a steady rhythm to your horse's gait, which encourages relaxation in the horse and always improves any situation.

The mantra also needs to be phrased positively—that is, describing what you want to do, not what you don't want to do. Rather than, "Don't lean," for example, you can say, "Sit tall." This is important, because the brain can't process a negative; instead, it has to picture the thing (leaning), and then decide what to do instead of that thing.

 ## Exercise: How to Get Rid of a Purple Elephant

1 For the next 30 seconds, *don't think* of a purple elephant. Don't think about anything related to the color purple or anything to do with a big, wrinkly creature with huge ears and a long trunk.

So, how did that go? If you're like most people, a big old grape-colored elephant just sauntered into the room, and you had to figure out what to do to get it to leave. You had to picture the thing in order not to picture it.

2 Now, for another 30 seconds, *think* of a white bear.

There. Much easier, right? You didn't have to get rid of one thought and replace it with a different thought; you could just focus on the thing you wanted to think about. Just phrasing your mantra as a "Do" rather than a "Don't do" removes a lot of mental clutter: you just have one thought in your brain instead of a "don't do that" thought *and* a "do this instead" thought.

The last feature of a mantra is that it should have a positive domino effect: following the mantra should allow everything else to fall into place. When I'm about to jump a log over a ditch (SCARY for me), I need to sit tall, keep my leg on, keep a strong pace, and not pick at my horse's stride (which is what my Lizard Brain wants to do, since it's a perfectionist with a ditch phobia). My mantra at those jumps is simply, "Keep coming, keep coming." If I do that, all of the other details fall right into place.

In a dressage test, I usually have one mantra the whole time, since things happen in quick succession; on my nervous Thoroughbred, it's usually, "Soft and through, soft and through," or something similar to that.

Your mantra is unique to you and your horse, and you may have a variety of them to fit various situations. Make sure that your mantras fit the emotional state in which you work best: if you need to stay peaceful, your mantra should match that mood, for example, "Light and easy, light and easy." If you're really going for it when you go in the ring, the mantra might be, "Big and bold, big and bold." You may also want to change your mantras over time, as old ones get stale or become obsolete.

Exercise: Mantras

On your piece of paper, list one or two mantras that you can use in challenging riding situations. First jot down the situation, then your mantra.

Next time you go riding, choose a mantra for your situation and use it for a few minutes.

MADDIE'S STORY: **"CHANNEL WILLIAM!"**

My 11-year-old student, Maddie, is in the middle of a major growth spurt, and she has a really tough time coordinating her rapidly changing and elongating body parts. She also idolizes top event rider William Fox-Pitt, who is long and lanky, as she is becoming. I can tell her, "Stretch your legs down, keep your elbows soft, make your hands stay still and quiet," which she tries very hard to do. But if I say, "Channel William," she immediately sits 4 inches taller and her body gets quiet and soft. I've done this with many riders, myself included, and I'm always amazed at the instant transformation.

Channeling

My third strategy for maintaining Focused Calm is to channel my favorite rider. Picture a séance being led by a medium. When the medium contacts someone who has died, she "channels" that person—speaks her words, uses the same inflection and body gestures, essentially becomes the person she's channeling. (Think Whoopie Goldberg's character in the movie *Ghost*.) Likewise, you can channel a rider you admire and "become" that rider.

Exercise: Channel Your Favorite Rider

Try this:

1 Before you get on your horse for your next ride, choose a rider you admire. It might be someone famous, it might be your trainer, or it might be the bubbly teenager at your barn who always has a great position and a huge grin on her face. It just needs to be someone who possesses a skill or trait that you would like to develop.

2 Picture that person riding as vividly as you can; even better, watch them on video or in person if possible.

3 When you settle into your saddle, channel that rider right into your body, and ride as that person. If you hit a snag, pause, visualize what that rider would do, and then channel that ride through your body.

4 Take a moment here to write some observations of what you felt during this exercise. What did it feel like to ride while channeling the person you admire? What did your body feel like? What was your mind doing? How did your horse respond? If you lost the channel at some point (as we all do), what changed in you and in your horse?

Are you having trouble thinking of someone you want to channel? Try watching more riding. Watch other lessons at your barn, watch a local show, or use that amazing creation that gives us access to any image we want: YouTube. You can get all the visual input you need in a two or three minute video, whether it's watching Buck Brannaman teach someone to bombproof their trail horse or seeing Charlotte Dujardin perform perfect canter pirouettes. Really stare at the action, and channel it the next time you're in the saddle. You can even sit on the edge of your chair and channel the person as you watch.

Channeling can also work in reverse: you can channel yourself into a rider you are watching. This is great for the times when you can't ride. Just choose a video of a rider you admire and channel yourself right into her body, right into the scene. As I write this, it's three degrees outside—no riding will be happening for me today! So instead, my trainer has ordered me to watch videos of German show jumper Marcus Ehning, and I'll channel myself into him as he jumps with invisible aids and seamless adjustments. I'm a terrible micro-manager, so channeling myself into Mr. Smooth-and-Seamless will give me a "feel" for what I should be doing instead.

ANY TIME, ANY PLACE

Focused Calm is one of those skills that can be practiced any time, any place. As you go through your day—at work, at home with your family, at the barn, with your friends—notice whether you are in Focused Calm. If not, pause for a moment, take a couple of soup breaths, and bring yourself into the present moment. Delete any distracting thoughts. Get into Performance Self if the situation calls for it, or step fully into your Real Self when you are spending time with people and animals you love.

The more fully present you can be in all parts of your life, the easier it will be to become calm and focused during your rides. Conversely, as you become more skilled at slipping into Focused Calm with your horse, you will probably notice that you are able to be more present in other areas of your life as well.

StressLess Practice:
How to Get Better (At Anything) Faster

Now that you're getting skilled at putting yourself into a state of Focused Calm, it's time to use that skill to help you improve both your riding and your confidence. In this chapter, I will share strategies from top performers in many areas that allow them to improve both their skills and their mental toughness, in ways that achieve results more quickly than most other methods can. As is often the case, a lot of this is going to feel counterintuitive, but for now, just roll along with me.

PRACTICE MAKES...MISTAKES?

Everyone has heard the old adage, "Practice makes perfect." Then, somewhere along the way, someone upped the ante on us and said, "Practice doesn't make perfect; *perfect* practice makes perfect." The theory goes that if you keep making mistakes in your practice, your performance never gets any better. This seems to make perfect sense— except for the minor detail that according to the latest research in neuroscience, it turns out to be completely wrong.

Let me clarify: it's true that sloppy, careless practice produces sloppy results. It's a waste of time to ride endless 20-meter circles if you ignore the quality of those circles, and repeating the same mistake over and over makes you really good at that mistake. However, endless "perfect" 20-meter circles don't necessarily make you a better rider, either. There is a time and place for perfection, but there is also a time and place for big, huge, awkward mistakes.

"Perfect practice makes perfect" is true when you are working to maintain or fine-tune a skill you have already mastered. If your goal for the day is to polish your horse's shoulder-in, and it's already solid to begin with, then your aim should be perfect practice. Perfect practice is also an appropriate goal right before a show: you aren't trying to learn or teach your horse something new, you just want to review the skills you'll need on the weekend to make them as strong and sparkling as possible.

When it comes to learning new skills or taking your current ones to a higher level, however, perfect practice is both unattainable *and undesirable.* If you've never done a flying change before, when you first start to learn how, you're going to miss—a lot. You might hit a streak of beginner's luck, and that's great, but it's not the same thing as mastery. In order to truly master a skill, you have to make lots and lots of mistakes, and then correct those mistakes, getting closer and closer to performing the skill correctly.

This process can be maddeningly slow and incredibly frustrating. The good news is that the more you make mistakes and correct them, the more your brain is learning and integrating the parts of the skill into its *neurological* memory. (What we usually call "muscle memory" is actually neurological memory: we develop neural pathways that command our muscles to perform the tasks that we want.)

If you normally post at the trot, think back to when you first learned this skill. At first, you probably bounced all over the place. You might have come up out of the saddle on every third or fourth stride, then banged roughly down on the saddle, where you bounced around some more. Your leg slipped forward, it slipped back, you fell forward, you got left behind. Eventually, you found the right rhythm, let the horse's movement toss you out of the saddle, sat back down without thumping, and voila! Up, down, up, down—you could post! This process might have taken hours or months, but you eventually mastered the skill.

During that process, the neurons in your brain were busily developing the network that would eventually become your "posting trot neural network." With each repetition, the neurons fired to make your seat go up and down. The more those neurons fired, the thicker they became. As you exerted effort to correct your mistakes and refine your movements, those neural pathways got stronger, and they developed more connections to other related neural pathways. For example, your "stand-up" neurons developed connections to your "hands-still" neurons. Eventually, you acquired a strong, integrated "posting trot" neural network that now functions more or less automatically.

For reasons we don't yet fully understand, it appears that effort, error, and correction of error are all essential in the process of this neural pathway development. In other words, you can't get better without screwing up a lot and working hard to fix it. Yes, some things come more easily than others, but in general, the acquisition of new and better skills is achieved in six steps:

1 Try.
2 Fail.
3 Figure out what went wrong.
4 Try again.
5 Fail better.
6 Repeat until mastery is achieved.

It's vital in this process to operate on the very *top edge* of your current ability. If the task isn't hard enough, the brain won't have to work to strengthen the neural network for that skill. On the other hand, if it's too far beyond your current capabilities, you won't be able to improve either, because you are over-faced and don't have a good foundation to build on.

If I ask you to try flying changes before you have even learned to canter, you're guaranteed to fail. It's like lifting weights: if you don't have to expend any effort to lift the weight, your muscles won't develop, but if you try to lift way too much, you'll fail completely. You need to lift an amount that's hard, but not impossible, in order to get stronger.

The Sweet Spot of Learning

In his outstanding book *The Talent Code*, author Daniel Coyle describes finding the "sweet spot" on the very edge of your abilities. This is the optimum place to spend the majority of your practice time: the place where you can try something, make mistakes, go back and correct those mistakes over and over, until you master the skill. (When you finish this book, read *The Talent Code.* It's the best book I have ever read on how to get better at anything. Plus, it gives you hope when you weren't born with Olympic-level genes.)

The sweet spot of learning is a frustrating place to be sometimes, because it feels awkward and takes a tremendous amount of concentration and effort. However, it's also the place where your greatest gains will be achieved. Sometimes the process is slow and painstaking, but at other times, there's a moment where everything just "clicks," and you make a quantum leap forward. In any case, take the awkwardness not as an indication that you're clumsy and hopeless, but as a sign that you're in the right place and practicing the right thing.

Feeling awkward is much easier for children than it is for adults. Think about it: when we were kids, we were beginners at most things, and experts at almost nothing. We tried, failed, and tried again at dozens of things every day. We fell off our bikes, we wrote our names in horrible, illegible handwriting, we tried to say "spaghetti" and it came out "basgetti." Awkward was a normal state of being. I watch my six year old nephew try new things, like ice skating, and it never occurs to him to feel self-conscious about struggling with it. He might get frustrated at times, but he doesn't get embarrassed by his awkwardness.

As adults, we are experts at so many things in our lives, and we are rarely in situations that require such determined practice. For many of us, riding is the only place in our lives where we have to expend such deliberate effort and experience mistakes on such a regular basis. Awkwardness not only feels hard, it often feels foolish. We get embarrassed when we are struggling with something and someone else in the arena is riding around, doing it effortlessly. We forget that they had to struggle to get there, too. (Remember the Inside/Outside Brain Trap of comparing your insides to other people's outsides?) Delete any thoughts from your Committee that tell you to bail because you're obviously hopeless, and train yourself to remember that the awkwardness is a sign that you're on the right track. Even the willingness to look foolish gets easier with practice!

Basketball legend Michael Jordan is reported to have said the following about failure and mistakes: "I've missed more than 9000 shots in my career. I've lost almost 300 games. Twenty-six times, I've been trusted to take the game winning shot and missed. I've failed over and over and over again in my life. And that is why I succeed" (see www. brainyquote.com). The God of Basketball, it turns out, wasn't born that way; he had to try and fail, and try again and fail better, right up until the end of his career, just like the rest of us. The best in any sport get there partly because they are more willing than the average person to risk looking ridiculous in order to get better.

Make Better Mistakes
When it comes to practice, some mistakes are better than others. As I mentioned earlier, repeating the same mistake again and again makes

you an expert at doing it wrong. This is how bad habits develop. So if you find yourself repeating the same error over and over, if your trainer keeps saying the same exact things in every lesson, it's time to make a different mistake. The simplest way to do this is to do the *exact opposite* of what you have been doing. If you usually tense your body when you sit the trot or jog, make yourself so floppy that you feel like you're going to slide off your horse. (Use a grab strap if you need to.) If you lean too far forward when you jump, get left way behind (just be sure to slip the reins so you don't catch your horse in the mouth). *Really exaggerate* doing the opposite, and then work your way back to the middle, and you'll end up doing the skill properly.

The flip side of doing the opposite is to make your usual mistake on purpose. Do you lean at the jumps? Lean waaaaay forward. (Keep the jumps small so you don't get dumped!) Do you hold the reins too loosely? Let them slide through your fingers until you're on the buckle or knot of the reins. Does this sound stupid? Of course—why would anyone want to make a problem worse? Well, for two reasons: one, to bring your awareness to it, and two, to develop control over it. If you can make it worse, you can also make it better. Remember, Focus is key to good performance, so anything that helps you zero in on a problem will help you to solve it.

Go Deep: Get the Most Out of Every Practice Minute

Now that you have some ideas for breaking bad habits, let's talk about preventing them from developing in the first place. When you put your foot in the stirrup at the start of your ride, do you have a plan for what you're going to work on and how you're going to work on it? The "what" is usually easier than the "how." How do you make the most of your (usually limited) saddle time so that you make as much improvement as possible during each ride? According to *The Talent Code,* it's by using something called Deep Practice.

Deep Practice is a strategy that Coyle discovered in places he calls "talent hotbeds"—places that consistently turn out superstars, such as Brazilian soccer programs. It involves the try-fail-try-fail-better sequence that I discussed earlier (see p. 87), used in a very deliberate way.

Deep Practice, according to Coyle, involves breaking skills down into small chunks, slowing everything down, stopping when you catch a mistake, analyzing what went wrong, and repeating the exercise with a focus on eliminating that mistake. You repeat this process, then repeat it again, and again. This happens over hours, weeks, and months, and at times it may feel like you're emptying the ocean with an eyedropper. But eventually, all of the chunks you have practiced intensely will come together in a smooth execution of the skill.

One classic example of Deep Practice is the pursuit of the Holy Grail of jumping: finding the perfect takeoff spot, or "distance," to a jump. I learned (am still learning) to do this by cantering to a pole on the ground and counting down my last three strides. 3, 2, 1, jump. 3, 2, jump—damn, I was late. Start earlier. 3, 2, 1, oops, jump—started too early. 3, 2, break to trot—nope, I was on the half stride. 3, 2, 1, jump—nailed it. And so on.

This practice, done in a state of Focused Calm, was then applied to a tiny crossrail, then to a small vertical, then an oxer, then the jumps got bigger, then we added combinations and turns and bending lines... and so on and so forth, until I now have a pretty consistent eye for a distance. I still miss, but I miss about 75 percent less often than I used to. Breaking the skill into smaller chunks helped me learn the whole picture more quickly in the long run.

According to Deep Practice rules, when you make a mistake, stop immediately and take a moment to analyze what went wrong. This step is vital to the process: you can't get better if you don't understand thoroughly what you are doing wrong. Make a specific, deliberate plan for what to do next, and then execute your plan. Again, stop if you make a mistake, and repeat until you've made progress on the skill.

Let me emphasize that last point: *repeat until you've made progress,* not until you have done something perfectly. Deep Practice is very intense and it can tire you and your horse quickly, so don't push to the point of diminishing returns. Also, make sure you praise your horse for his efforts, don't just correct his mistakes. He needs to know what he is doing right, and he needs to feel good about his work.

When you are tempted to do "just one more thing," remember that good horsemanship requires all of us to know when to say, "Good boy!" and call it a day. Incessant drilling and an overemphasis on perfection lead to sour, resentful horses (and people, for that matter).

You will probably find that 20 to 30 minutes of Deep Practice will lead to better mastery for both of you than an hour of less targeted exercises. Give you and your horse plenty of breaks during your ride as well, to give both of you a chance to process what you've done and to regroup for the next round. I like to mix up Deep Practice and Perfect Practice, ending with things that are relatively easy for my horse and me, so we can finish feeling positive and motivated to continue next time.

COMFORTABLE...DISCOMFORT?

To be a strong, confident equestrian athlete, it isn't enough to Deep Practice just the physical skills of riding. You also have to develop the ability to tolerate risk and failure, and the skill to bounce back from setbacks and disappointment. There are a variety of words to describe this ability, but my favorite is *resilience.* Resilient people are strong but flexible; they get knocked down seven times, so they get up eight times. Failures and setbacks bother them (a lot!), but instead of being defeated by them, resilient riders use these experiences to become stronger than before. The quote on page 89 from Michael Jordan is an illustration of resilience, taken all the way to the top of his chosen field.

I believe that as riders, we need resilience even more than many other athletes, given the unpredictability and fragility of our equine partners. If champion downhiller Bode Miller's ski gets cracked, he grabs his spare skis. However, if my horse comes out of his stall three-legged lame on competition morning, I'm out of luck, and I'll be sitting watching my friends instead of joining them in the warm-up. We have to find ways to bounce back from these hard knocks, to avoid getting dragged down by them and instead use them to our advantage somehow.

Some people seem to be blessed with a sunny personality or an easy tolerance for disappointment and failure (especially public failure). These people drive me crazy, and I think they are really aliens from another planet. Most of us humans have to work at it. A lot. Moving up to the next level of competition, taking your horse to a new environment, and trying a new riding discipline are all examples of situations where you are taking emotional as well as physical risks. As a result, these experiences often produce a lot of anxiety for riders. "What if I fail? What if my horse is a lunatic? What if I make a total idiot of myself?"

As I mentioned in chapter 1, your Lizard Brain doesn't know the difference between an emotional risk and a saber-toothed tiger, so new challenges can often feel very intimidating even if the physical danger is minimal. So how do you become less afraid, more comfortable with those challenges? How do you learn to be more resilient, more confident? The answer is very simple: Put. Yourself. Out. There.

I said this at a workshop entitled, "Who, Me? Move Up?" and a collective, frustrated sigh came from the participants. Everyone there was hoping I held the secret to *feeling* confident *before* doing something hard or scary, that somehow I could get them off the hook and out of feeling the awkward, squirmy discomfort of the experience. Nope. I wish I could—I could have written a much shorter book, gotten obscenely rich, and gone shopping for an Olympic horse by now, which

I would confidently take to the Olympics with no discomfort whatsoever. But alas, the road to confidence goes directly down Do The Scary Thing Street. No detours, do not pass Go, do not collect $200.

Before you get completely disgusted with me, though, here's the good news: you don't have to go right out and do The Biggest Scary Thing. You can do just a Slightly Scary Thing, and then another, and another, until the Biggest Scary Thing doesn't feel so big anymore. Essentially, you're Deep Practicing courage!

Feel Uncomfortable—And Do It Anyway

You probably have done this with physically and emotionally scary things in your riding already: you trotted before you cantered, you trotted over a pole before you jumped, you did the lowest division in your first show before you moved up to a higher level at the next one. You've also done it in your regular life: you said hi to your crush in the hallway at school, you went to your first job interview, you gave a speech in front of your class or church group or board of directors. In the same spirit, this next step is about gaining greater confidence by intentionally taking progressively more difficult emotional and mental risks, and showing your Lizard Brain that you lived to tell the tale.

We discussed in chapter 2 how to calm your Lizard Brain by offering it reassurance and a plan: "It's okay, we will survive this, and here's what we're going to do." Putting Yourself Out There is the execution of that plan: it's time to stop thinking about it and go out and do it. All the reassurance and planning in the world won't take away 100 percent of the anxiety. Becoming more confident isn't really about feeling less uncomfortable in challenging situations; it's about *becoming more comfortable with being uncomfortable.*

When we want to take a step forward in our lives, most of us make the mistake of believing we must *feel* ready in order to *be* ready. Unfortunately, our Lizard Brains are rarely ready to stay relaxed about something new—after all, if we've never done it before, we don't know where the tigers are hiding, so vigilance must be maintained! If we wait for our Inner Lizards to be comfortable, we'll never do anything truly challenging. This may feel safe, but it also leads to a pretty bland, colorless life. Achieving growth and progress means accepting a level of discomfort and forging ahead anyway.

Your Lizard Brain will probably hate this at first, and it will probably tell you a whole bunch of scary stories about the awful things that will happen if you venture out into this unknown territory. That's fine. That's just the Lizard doing its job. You can respond with a simple, two sentence mantra: "It's just a little discomfort. It can't hurt me." Once you've gently reassured your Lizard that no one is going to die, move forward and do what you set out to do.

After you've put yourself out there, notice the results. Notice that whether you succeeded or failed, you are still here. Notice that you survived your discomfort, and notice whether it really was as bad as you thought it was going to be. Regardless of the end result, you did it—you put yourself out there. *That is a success in and of itself.*

The more you put yourself in uncomfortable situations, the less the discomfort will bother you. The more your Lizard sees that discomfort isn't fatal, the less it will need to call out the cavalry every time you venture into uncharted territory. Authors Katty Kay and Claire Shipman put it beautifully in their book, *The Confidence Code*: "Confidence occurs when the insidious self-perception that you aren't able is trumped by the stark reality of your achievements" (p. 50).

You have probably already noticed that putting yourself out there is an important skill in every facet of life. Every time you do it in one area, you boost your overall confidence in yourself, and you can bring that confidence to bear in other areas. You probably already have more experience with this than you realize.

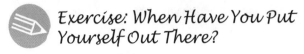

Exercise: When Have You Put Yourself Out There?

Take a moment to answer the following questions:
When was the last time you did something new or different, something that made you slightly (or very) uncomfortable? Changed jobs, moved, took your child to preschool, or to college? *Everything counts*, even something as simple as driving somewhere you've never been or trying oysters on the half shell for the first time.

- What did you tell yourself to convince yourself to do it?

- How did you feel afterward? How do you feel now about doing it again?

- Did you survive? (Remember, this is *not* a stupid question from your Lizard's point of view.)

When you recognize that you have been uncomfortable before and lived to tell the tale, it's a little less threatening to do it again, especially if the payoff is greater confidence in your riding. The more you intentionally practice getting comfortable with being uncomfortable, the less uncomfortable it actually becomes!

You can practice physical discomfort as well as emotional discomfort. Below are some exercises for getting over being awkward, both emotionally and physically. Choose a couple of them, and after doing each one, notice what happened, and notice how you feel.

Exercise: Getting Comfortable with Discomfort

1 Switch-hitting: Brush your teeth and hair, brush your horse, muck a stall, tighten your girth, all with your non-dominant hand.

2 In line at the grocery store, ask someone to hold your jacket while you look for your keys.

3 Ride for 10 minutes with one stirrup, or with one stirrup 4 holes longer than the other.

4 Walk up to a more advanced rider you've never met, and ask a question.

5 Ride a pattern—a dressage test, jump course, reining pattern—then ride it in reverse order.

6 Say no to someone who asks you to do something you don't want to do, and don't apologize.

7 Go out in public and do something that is against the social norm. Nothing illegal or immoral, just something no one would expect.

Keep practicing until that Really Scary Thing—cantering off the longe line, riding through an open field, moving up a level, trying a new discipline or activity—feels like a Slightly Scary Thing, then go and do it. You and your Lizard will feel more confident on the other side. In fact, you'll probably feel amazing.

CAITLIN'S STORY: "CAN I HAVE A BITE?"

A college friend of mine, Caitlin, took Sociology 101 during freshman year. Her first homework assignment was Number 7 above: Do something in public that is outside the social norm. Some people walked into an elevator and stood facing the back wall; other people went into a mostly empty movie theater and sat in the seat that was right next to another person. Caitlin went up to someone eating an ice cream cone and asked them for a bite of ice cream. The students were supposed to report on the reactions of others, but Caitlin said it had the side benefit of proving to her that no one ever dies of embarrassment!

HANDY SURVIVAL SKILLS

The horse's flight instinct is a major cause of the problems that lead to damaged confidence. Spooks, spins, bolts, and bucks can all leave us on the ground, and leave our courage in tatters. If you have tools for dealing with these behaviors, though, you'll feel more in control and less at the mercy of your horse's Lizard Brain. Here are a few strategies for handling some common behaviors.

 Riding Exercise: Spooking—"Own" His Eyeballs

When you control your horse's line of sight, you can control his attention. If he tends to spook at a mailbox or a particular corner of the ring, "own" his eyeballs! *You* get to choose what he pays attention to.

1 Flex his jaw and neck away from the spooky object with one rein, so that he can't stare at it. Use your leg to help bend him away from the object. So, if the object is on his right, use your left leg and left rein to bend him away from it. This may be difficult at first; don't yank or kick, but be persistent and firm.

2 As you bend him, exhale and soften your seat and arms. This sends the message, "Everything is fine." If you tense up, this tells him that you see a tiger somewhere—and if you're worried, he should be too!

3 If you can, start bending him before you get close to the spooky thing; it's easier to prevent a problem than to solve one.

4 If he's gawking and spooking at the world in general, it's likely that he is more distracted than afraid. Give him a job so that you have a place to focus his attention: move him sideways or make small circles, lengthen and shorten his stride, do transitions from walk to trot to halt—anything that brings his attention back to you.

From my point of view, there is a difference between a distracted or habitual spook (it's always in the same corner of the arena, or anytime one of the dogs goes running by), and a spook that's about genuine fear. Let me tell you about Max.

MY STORY: **ATTENTION DEFICIT DISORDER**

I have a lovely Irish Draught horse named Max in training. He's an absolute sweetheart who would climb into your pocket if you let him. He's a lovely, floaty mover; he feels like sitting on a couch. I call him my "ego ride," because even on an off day, he makes me look good!

However, Max also has a raging case of Attention Deficit Disorder. He's constantly looking around and spooking at silly things—a squirrel, the cows that are there every day, a leaf blowing by. He's not really scared, so much as astonished at the world: "Hey, look! There are cows! Did you see that leaf? Who put that jacket there? Did you know that the sand makes a funny noise when it hits the wall of the indoor?"

I spend a *lot* of time owning his eyeballs.

One day, however, when there was a big blue tarp sitting next to the arena, blowing a little in the breeze, he was genuinely (and understandably) afraid of it. It hadn't been there before, so his Lizard Brain was warning him that a tiger might be lurking underneath it. In that case, I made him walk up and check it out for a couple of minutes. Once he knew it wouldn't eat him, we went back to work. After that, if he wanted to spook at the tarp, I did the Own His Eyeballs exercise to get him back on track. Fear and distraction are two very different creatures that need different responses.

Riding Exercise: How to Stop a Speeding Train—The Pulley Rein

As I've discussed, horses are flight animals, and sooner or later you are likely to have a horse bolt away with you. In this situation, just pulling back on the reins won't be effective in getting him to stop. A pulley rein can stop a horse by using the leverage of your body weight. If you are neck reining, you will need to switch so that you take one rein in each hand. The instructions are for a right-handed person; if you're left-handed, reverse the hand positions.

1 Push your feet down and forward—think "Feet on the dashboard." Lean back with your shoulders behind your hips.

2 Holding the left rein, press your left hand firmly on the withers. This gives you a leverage point and helps to stabilize your balance.

3 With your right hand, give a sharp tug on the rein, but tug straight up with your hand above the horse's neck, not back toward your body. (Think "turn your wrist to the sky," and keep tugging upward.) It is much harder for the horse to lock his jaw and neck against you this way. You may need to put a fair amount of force into this and tug several times. Because it is quite intense, this is a strategy that you only use in a true runaway situation.

The same position is also effective with a horse that bucks. In this case, get into pulley rein position, but add a kick to push his hind legs back underneath him as you tug upward to raise his head. When his head is up and his hind legs are under him, it's much harder for him to buck hard enough to unseat you.

To practice the pulley rein, just put your body in the correct position and pretend to tug upward on the rein. It's unfair to do a real pulley rein on a horse that is behaving himself just fine!

Handling Terrain and Speed

If you trail ride, foxhunt, event, or otherwise ride outside an enclosed arena, dealing effectively with terrain is an essential skill. Learning to trot and canter downhill will prepare you to handle almost any situation out in the open. Even if you normally ride in an enclosed area, this exercise is a wonderful one to try—it's an instant confidence-builder!

 Riding Exercise: The Man from Snowy River

(If you don't know what this title refers to, go to Netflix and watch the movie, "The Man from Snowy River." There's a fantastic scene where the cowboy rides down a bank so steep it's almost a cliff. It's a classic!)

1 Find a hill, the steeper the better, with good footing.

2 Tie a knot in the end of your reins. Now sit tall, hold onto the knot, and go down the hill *without pulling on the reins*. Your feet should feel slightly out in front of you, but not as dramatically as when you did a pulley rein.

3 Start at the walk if you like, and work your way up to trot and canter, until eventually you can gallop down the hill, holding onto the knot, with a big loop in the reins.

4 You can squeeze on the reins momentarily to control his speed, but always release afterward, so he can use his neck for balance.

This scared the daylights out of me the first time I did it! However, I quickly realized that when I looped the reins, my horse could use his neck to help him balance himself down the hill. Pulling on the reins actually made it harder for him to keep his balance, and he would speed up to compensate. Now, I maintain contact when I gallop downhill, but I soften my hand to allow my horse to use his neck for balance.

It may take several sessions for you to work up to cantering down the hill, and that's fine. Take as long as you need. Just be sure to notice that letting go actually works, so that you can begin to trust it.

Riding Exercise: Look, Ma, No Hands!

Learn to balance in the saddle while completely letting go of the reins.

1 Start out in an enclosed space, or a familiar one where you and your horse are comfortable.

2 First at the walk, then at the trot, and eventually at the canter, practice dropping your reins for several strides, and then picking them back up again.

3 Work to deepen your seat and stay balanced for longer and longer periods of time (use the reins to steer as much as necessary, but keep dropping them in between).

4 When this becomes easy, start doing it without your stirrups. If you can stay balanced without reins and stirrups, you can sit most spook-and-spin maneuvers, no matter how fast your horse is!

Survival Strategies for Jumping

You may think that leaping over obstacles on horseback is the best thing ever. Your Lizard Brain, however, is thinking, "Who thought *this* was a good idea?!?" Here are some exercises to help you stick in the tack when things go awry.

Riding Exercise: Ride Ugly

Ugly, messy jumps are inevitable. You get in badly to a fence, the horse trips or spooks, whatever—sometimes things just go to hell in a handbasket. The key is to stay in balance and get out of your horse's way so that he can get the job done, and you can regroup on the other side of the jump.

I learned this exercise from Lucinda Green, who is one of the top cross-country riders in the world, and the Queen of Get It Done. It will teach you to get out of your horse's way, and it will teach your horse to mind his own feet and be responsible for his own balance.

1 Take five or six jump rails and put them down at random distances in a zig-zag line. If possible, use skinny rails, but full-sized ones will work. Do *not* measure the distances!

2 Build these into small jumps, not more than 12 to 18 inches high to begin with. Start even smaller if you like.

3 Now, trot into the line and jump the fences, but stay seated in the saddle, lean back a little, and slip your reins so you don't catch your horse in the mouth.

4 Widen your hands to steer your horse down the line of jumps (as if you're pushing a wheelbarrow).

Do *not* try to find a distance—let the horse figure that out.

This will feel messy, ugly, and awkward—and that is the whole point! This is meant to replicate situations where things have gone completely wrong, and the goal is to Get. It. Done. Eventually, you will be able to follow the horse more smoothly, but once it starts to feel "pretty," mix up the distances or raise the jumps to keep practicing how to cope with "ugly." This skill has saved my bacon more times than I can count, in all kinds of situations.

For a wonderful example of how "riding ugly" can save a situation, check out the video of American show jumper Richard Spooner at https://www.youtube.com/watch?v=gtv2sK6jbp4 (or type "Richard Spooner no reins" into the YouTube search box). He rides in completely wrong to an enormous combination of three jumps in a row, and the horse goes straight through the rails of the first fence, scattering them like pickup sticks. He drops the reins, throws his arms out to the sides for balance, and sits back, and his horse proceeds to jump the second two jumps of the combination. He picks up the reins on the other side and finishes the course!

Keep It Uncomfortable

Practice as many awkward situations as you can think of: Drop one stirrup before you go over a jump, then pick it up on the other side. Drop the reins in the air and get them back on landing. Practice preventing refusals: sit tall, put the reins in one hand, and pretend to use your crop behind the saddle.

All of these things will help you develop the reflex of staying in balance and getting the job done when something doesn't go according to plan.

Don't Punish Your Horse

In practice situations, always keep the jumps on the low side, so that you can just focus on practicing the skill. Also, avoid catching your horse in the mouth or banging down on his back; you don't want him to feel punished during these exercises. I encourage people to use a neck strap and/or a breastplate so that there is something to grab besides the reins.

As you practice these survival skills, your confidence will grow because you'll know you have plenty of tools in your toolbox should a problem arise. Fewer and fewer of your horse's goofy and unexpected maneuvers will unseat you, and you'll learn to trust that ability to stick to the tack. Practice perfectly to perfect your skills, and Deep Practice to build new abilities, but don't be afraid to Ride Ugly when you need to!

StressLess Showing:
Competing with Confidence

At the 2000 Olympic Games in Sydney, Australia, a stadium full of spectators holds its breath. US rider David O'Connor has just looked left, then right, clearly unsure of which fence he is supposed to jump next. He suddenly remembers and makes a quick right turn. The crowd exhales in relief, David finishes with a clear round, and the Olympic gold medal is his.

On a crisp, sunny fall day, in the "grasshopper" division of a local schooling show, a 10-year-old girl on a gray pony gallops by at top speed, tricked out in bright orange and purple, an enormous grin on her face.

The Rolex Kentucky Three-Day Event, 2007: The crowd lets out a collective cry of dismay as first-placed rider Kristin Bachman jumps the wrong fence, eliminating her from the competition. She doesn't realize it at first—and then a look of utter devastation washes across her face.

At a tiny schooling show in midsummer, an adult amateur finishes her first-ever dressage test, salutes the judge, and throws her arms around her horse's neck with a beaming smile and tears in her eyes.

Ah, horse shows—roller coasters of anxiety and elation, excitement and disappointment. No matter what level you are riding, no matter what your discipline is, if you show, I'm guessing you know exactly what I'm talking about.

Successful showing demands long hours of hard work and

preparation, not to mention significant financial and emotional investment. Most adult riders have to juggle work schedules, child care, family needs, and many other commitments to find the time to prepare and compete. It's understandable, then, that riders want not only to be successful at shows, but to genuinely enjoy the experience as well—otherwise, why go through all of those hassles and stressors?

This chapter discusses how to manage the inherent stress and anxiety of competition so that showing becomes a positive, fulfilling experience. I will take you through the process of effective preparation, and then address the skills required for effective showing—most of which aren't specific to riding at all, as you will see!

DEFINING SUCCESS

Success: *noun* The favorable or prosperous termination of attempts or endeavors; the accomplishment of one's goals (Dictionary.com).

What constitutes a successful show season? Well, that depends. It might mean winning a place on the US Equestrian Team, or qualifying for the Young Rider Championships. It might involve earning your bronze medal in dressage, or moving up to the amateur/owner division in the jumpers. However, it may also mean remembering your test at your first show, riding in your first Western Pleasure class, or making it around your first hunter course. Success is a very personal, individual concept, and it's extremely important to define it for yourself, based on who you are, where you are in the training process, and where you are in your life at this moment.

Imagine yourself at Thanksgiving dinner this November. Someone asks if you had a good show season, and you answer that yes, it was very successful. Knowing very little about horses, the person asks, "What made it so good?" How will you answer this question? In other words, how will you know that you've had a good year?

Exercise: What Is a Successful Show Season?

On a handy piece of paper or your tablet, write your answer in as much detail as you can.

I know I have had a successful show season because....

Answering this question sets your goals for your show season. Unfortunately, many people either skip this step entirely or don't know how to do it effectively, and this can lead to confusion and disappointment. Even if your goal is simply "to have fun showing my horse," it helps to know what that means for you. You view a situation positively or negatively mainly based upon your expectations of that situation; your goals clarify those expectations. If your goal at a show is to be in the top three in order to qualify for a regional competition, you'll view fifth place as a failure; however, if the goal was to complete your first show, you'll be thrilled with fifth place!

Effective goals help to set your path in the training process, like choosing a destination on a map. You decide where you want to go, and then you identify the route you need to take to get there. Useful goals need to include several components.

Goals need to:

- Be inspiring.
- Ask you to reach, and are also realistic.
- Be customized to fit you and your horse.
- Be a mix of Outcome Goals and Process Goals (I'll explain what I mean on p. 110).
- Come with a plan for how to achieve them.
- Be flexible.

Inspiration

A goal needs to inspire you; it should get you fired up and excited! Otherwise, what's the point of all that hard work? Getting inspired means challenging yourself, pushing yourself beyond that peaceful comfort zone, and reaching for the next level. If your goal doesn't scare you just a little bit, it's probably too easy!

Being inspired does not necessarily mean feeling 100 percent ready to take on your new challenge. Remember, perfectionism is a trap that holds you back from what you can become. Don't wait until you *feel* ready, with every little detail perfectly aligned and every minute skill mastered. Ride safely, but be willing to make mistakes on your way to reaching your goals. Every goal worth achieving requires a certain leap of faith at the beginning, a willingness to believe that you *can* get there, in spite of your doubts right at this moment. Don't let the fear of future failure stop you from reaching for your dreams right now.

As master performance coach Don Greene says, "You can't steal second with your feet on first."

Specific, Realistic, and Customized

Vague goals aren't really goals, they're stalling tactics. "I want to be a better rider," or "I want to perform well," are statements that let you off the hook—who can argue with wanting to be a better rider?—but they are pretty useless in the motivation department. Effective goals are specific: you can point to your actions as evidence that you have accomplished them. "I will sit the trot without bouncing," and "I will move up to First Level by August," are specific and tangible.

"I want to win the 4' Amateur-Owner Division in July," is specific all right, but is it realistic? Not if it's April and you've never jumped a three-foot jump before. Goals should be challenging, but they also need to match your reality. If you are working full time and have three kids all playing different sports, it may not be feasible to reach a goal of showing every other weekend. A student at our farm who is in her fourth year of medical school simply does not have the time to keep her horse fit to show at the same level she competed in college, so she has to adjust her expectations for herself and her horse this year.

Challenges come in all shapes and sizes. It's challenging to compete at the upper levels, but it's also a huge challenge, for example, to compete at any level in your discipline while holding down a full-time college course load. Horses are important, but so are your life and the people you care about. Your goals need to reflect what is realistic, given your current life circumstances.

I often see riders setting goals based on the rider they think they *should want to be*, rather than the rider they *are right now*. Suppose you have a horse that is capable of doing the 3'6" hunters, and several other riders in your barn are excitedly preparing their horses for that division. However, the idea of jumping that high scares the living daylights out of you; just the thought of it makes you queasy. Still, you feel like you "should" want it. After all, everyone else seems excited about it, and you know your horse can do it, so what's your problem?

Here's your problem: *absolutely nothing.* There is nothing wrong with saying, "That's not for me." We have so many disciplines and so many levels of difficulty in equestrian sport precisely because there are so many different personalities that comprise the riding population. Choose a level and type of competition that suits who you are and makes you happy.

"But," a rider said to me once, "my horse has so much potential. People say I'm wasting his talent if I don't compete him to the higher levels. I feel like I'm letting him down if I don't go to the big shows."

I have heard this one on multiple occasions, usually from someone who had enough money to buy a really nice horse, but then had the "audacity" to want to simply experience the pleasure of riding this nice horse instead of collecting as many ribbons as possible at the highest possible level. Other people—trainers, friends, envious bystanders—see this pleasure as a "waste," because they are busy fantasizing about how they could meet *their* competitive goals with such a lovely horse. This, however, has absolutely nothing to do with anything.

Ideally, we choose our horses because we love how we feel when we ride them. If that experience includes competition at some level, that's great. But if not, that's equally wonderful. No one else's vote counts. And as for letting down your horse? I guarantee that he's not lying in his stall at night, staring at his Horses of the Olympics poster, thinking, "Man, if my stupid rider would just get her act together, I could be one of them someday!"

Conversely, if you *do* want to go to the Olympics, don't be deterred by others who tell you that you're too competitive or that you should just relax and have fun. These same people may tell you to be more "realistic" about your aspirations, and that you should avoid setting yourself up for disappointment. Avoiding disappointment might be safe, but it's also letting yourself down if you have high aspirations and big dreams. Again, the vote that counts most is your own. You are the one doing the work to achieve your dreams. There is no "right" way to approach showing; what matters is that your approach suits you and your horse.

Outcome Goals versus Process Goals

Outcome Goals are exactly what they sound like: you want to achieve a particular outcome or end result. Qualifying for the National Saddle Seat Equitation Championships or the Quarter Horse Congress, making the Young Riders Team, and earning a bronze medal in dressage are all examples of outcome goals.

Process Goals, on the other hand, don't depend upon a specific result. Instead, process goals focus on particular aspects of you and your horse's performance, regardless of your competitive results. Getting clean flying changes, jumping a course at a challenging height,

KELLY'S STORY: **GOOD VERSUS BAD GOALS**

Kelly had been riding school horses for quite awhile, and decided that for her fiftieth birthday, she was going to buy herself the horse of her dreams. Kelly worked at a lucrative job, so she was able to set a very generous budget to buy the horse, significantly more than the amounts that other boarders in her barn had spent on their horses. After a long search, she and her trainer found a horse that Kelly fell in love with, and she bought him.

While Kelly didn't share the purchase price with anyone, a few people looked up the horse online and discovered what his asking price had been, and word got around. They started asking Kelly whether she was going to aim the horse for the area championships in the fall.

After taking the horse to a couple of shows, Kelly discovered that while showing was kind of enjoyable, she didn't love it. What she loved, she found, was the process of learning to ride her new horse and the experience of having him as her own. She decided she would go to a few shows and enjoy the social aspect of them, but she didn't want the pressure of trying to qualify for anything.

Several people criticized Kelly for being "unmotivated" and for "wasting the horse's talent with just riding at home." She started second-guessing her purchase.

"Maybe I don't deserve such a nice horse, since I'm not going to show. I don't really need a horse of this caliber if I don't want to ride in the championships."

I pointed out to Kelly that 1) her horse didn't care, as long as she loved him and gave him a great life, and 2) she "deserved" the nicest horse that she could afford to buy, regardless of what she did with him.

There are not good goals and bad goals. Wanting to go to the Olympics is not inherently better than wanting to go trail riding. Horses couldn't care less about ribbons or trophies, and they don't know whether they are fancy or well-bred or talented. They would just as soon "waste" their talent eating grass in a pasture for the rest of their lives as bring home an Olympic gold medal!

and coping effectively with a green or spooky horse in the ring are all Process goals, accomplishments that can be celebrated regardless of how you placed at a particular show.

I believe strongly in having a mix of Outcome and Process goals. If you base your definition of success solely upon the outcomes of competition, you are setting yourself up for discouragement and feelings of failure. Too many variables come into play: it pours during your qualifying test and your young horse hates mud, you have an unlucky rail in a jump-off, your horse spooks in the middle of your ride and refuses to settle down again. And then there's the simple reality that sometimes, someone else's best day is better than your best day. All of these

MY STORY: **KEEPING EVERYTHING IN PERSPECTIVE**

I've had to keep myself very committed to my Process Goals recently. In the last couple of years I have just begun competing at the upper levels of eventing, and I am now a *very* tiny fish in a *very* large pond! Many riders in my divisions already wear U.S. Equestrian Team coats, and most have multiple horses at the upper levels, along with the sponsors to pay for it all.

I'm a newbie at these levels in my mid-forties; many of them rode Advanced before they were twenty-five. They got their beginner mistakes out of the way a long time ago; I'm smack in the middle of making those mistakes. If I focus only on the scoreboard, I can get demoralized pretty quickly. I need to keep my Process Goals at the forefront to remind me that I'm making progress. Knowing that I used my hands correctly in a stadium-jumping round or that our dressage was more settled than last time allows me to enjoy the competition, instead of worrying only about my placing at the end of the weekend.

elements are out of your control. If they are your only measuring stick, you're going to be miserable a lot of the time, and you won't have an accurate idea of how you're progressing.

Adding Process goals to the mix will give you some additional markers to measure your progress. You may not place in a class, but you nailed your flying changes, so you had a successful ride. You kept your spooky horse settled in the ring? It was a good day. You jumped around your first three-foot course? That's a success, regardless of where you ended up on the scoreboard. Outcome goals give you a wonderful rush of elation; Process goals, though, give you the lasting satisfaction of achieving higher and higher training milestones. Both experiences have their own particular value.

 Exercise: What Are Your Goals?

What are your goals for the current or next show season? Write them down and notice if they are mostly Outcome Goals, and if so, add some Process Goals to the mix.

THE PLAN: YOUR ROAD MAP TO ACHIEVEMENT

Setting goals is all fine and well, but if you're going to reach them, you need a plan. A good plan shows you clearly what you need to do in the next week, the next month, the next three months, and further out if necessary. It should include a schedule of shows you will attend, any lessons or clinics, and a list of skills that you need to work on in your day-to-day training. Include any special care your horse will need also, such as body work or specific vaccinations. Here is a sample plan for one of my students:

Sample Riding Plan

Date of plan: April 1

Goal: Ride in my first sanctioned dressage show on August 12

By the show date I need to:
• Master my leg-yields and counter-canter.
• Sit a trot lengthening.
• Choose and memorize the two dressage tests I will ride.

In the next three months I will:
• Do one schooling show per month.
• Take one lesson per week.
• Ride without stirrups two times per week.

This month I will:
• Study YouTube videos of upper-level dressage riders and
    focus on their positions.
• Join the required associations to go to the show.

This week I will:
• Ride for 10 minutes at a time without stirrups.
• Take a lesson on Tuesday.
• Send in the entry for this month's dressage show.

By working backward from your goal date, you can get down to the specific things you need to accomplish each week. This is especially helpful if your goal is a long way off, such as when you're planning your show season in the dead of winter!

 *Exercise: Write Out Your Own Goal and Detailed Plan*

Using the Sample Riding Plan on the previous page, make your plan.

Flexibility

If you haven't yet had your plan thwarted by a lost shoe, a truck break-down, or a fat leg (yours or your horse's), you just haven't been showing long enough. Sooner or later, we all have to make adjustments to our goals thanks to some unexpected occurrence. Horses are horses, and life is unpredictable, so we have to keep a flexible mindset about our goals and plans. Sometimes the need for adjustment will be obvious: your horse strains a suspensory ligament and is out for the remainder of the season. Other times, however, the need for flexibility won't be quite so clear-cut, which means that we have to pay attention and listen to our horse.

Usually, a goal is realistic when you set it. For example, your horse performed really well at shows last year, so this spring, you decide to move him up to the next level. However, as you ride in a couple of shows, you find that he is very anxious and is making a lot of tension-related mistakes. You may need to drop back to his previous level for a little while and let him regain his confidence before pressing forward. If he is getting stiff and sore after shows, you may need to work more on his fitness.

One of the risks of competition is becoming so focused on achieving success that you miss the signs that your partner is unhappy. It's vital that you continually evaluate your horse's well-being and comfort. Horses have different rates of development and different levels of stress toler-ance; just because one horse is ready for a particular level at age five doesn't mean that the next horse will automatically do the same. Some horses can show every weekend without a problem, but some horses get too stressed and develop ulcers or sore backs with this schedule, and need to compete less often. A flexible outlook on the training process is essential for long-term competitive success, as well as for the health of our horses.

Luck Favors the Prepared

In eventing, riders must walk their cross-country jumping course so they know the path to take and which fences to jump. A trainer I know once confessed to me that at age 14, doing her first event, she didn't know this—she thought she had to find her way as she went along! Fortunately, another rider set her straight, so she didn't end up lost in the woods for hours.

The moral of this story: know the drill before you go. Make sure you are familiar with the rules and etiquette of your chosen discipline. Read the Rule Book. (Yes, it's tedious. Read it anyway.) If possible, go to some shows as a spectator or groom to get a feel for the rhythm of the typical show day.

Being a spectator allows you to become familiar with the atmosphere without the stress of your own competition nerves. It also gives you the opportunity to observe successful riders and watch how they handle challenges, such as bad weather or an uncooperative horse. I especially like watching riders in the warm-up area, as this is usually the place where people either step successfully into Performance Self or escalate tension in themselves and their horses. When I see a rider who is completely in her Performance Self, I try to identify what she is doing to stay there in the midst of all the distractions around her.

Another benefit of watching is noticing that even the best riders aren't perfect all the time. I've seen every rider I admire make mistakes: they have refusals at jumps, they go off course in their dressage tests, their horses have meltdowns, they fall off. While I'm not hoping someone will make a mistake, when they do have a bobble, it reminds me that they're human too. As a result, when my turn comes, I can be less self-conscious about my own errors and stay better focused on the next task at hand.

Get Your Stuff Together

Riding is an equipment-heavy sport, to put it mildly. When I pack the truck for the weekend, my husband and I joke that the neighbors must think I'm moving out! Your stuff can be a source of stress or a source of confidence, depending on how you handle it.

Organization Is in the Eye of the One Who Has to Find Her Stuff

Organization is a very individual concept. One person's jumble is another person's system. I won't tell you how you should arrange your stuff; however, I strongly recommend that you have a system. Systems, like routines, are excellent stress relievers, because they reduce the need to think. When I need my gloves, I don't have to think about where I put them; I just reach into the front pocket of my garment bag, because that's where they always are. My system frees up mental space for more important things, and it's one less thing to stress about as I'm preparing to ride.

How do you know whether you have an effective system for your stuff? If you look at your arrangement and you feel calm, it's a good system. If you feel stressed or anxious when you look at it, you need to make some changes. My personal rule of thumb is that if I can't put my hands on something I need within 10 seconds, I need to adjust my system. In my house and in my office, I can handle a fair amount of chaos, but at a horse show, I need to start with everything in place, or I feel frazzled.

A note to parents and coaches: it is extremely tempting to impose a particular system on your child or student because it makes sense to you. However, it will only work if it makes sense to *them*. If they throw everything into their trunk in one big jumble, but they can find what they need when they need it, *leave it alone.* Walk away if you have to, but don't meddle with their stuff just because it's driving you crazy. If they can't find what they need, are chronically late, or are constantly asking you to go back for something they forgot, then you can intervene. Even then, however, don't just impose a system upon them; help them develop one that both of you can be comfortable with.

Lists: It Only Exists if It's Written Down Somewhere

Lists are another important tool to help manage your stuff. I have seen people forget saddles, riding boots—someone once told me they even forgot one of their ponies! My own memory is way too unreliable for me to work without lists. I have a generic packing list on my computer, and I print out a clean list every time I pack for a show or a clinic. I customize it for a particular show, if necessary. Every item on the list gets crossed off when, and only when, I put it in the truck or trailer. Even if the item lives in my travel trunk that never leaves the trailer, I make sure I see it in there before I cross it off the list. It's way too easy to grab the shampoo out of my travel trunk in between shows and forget to put it back, then arrive at the show and discover—yikes! No shampoo!

Again, this is my list strategy; you may have a different one that works for you. If it's working, don't change it. If you find that you often forget things, however, it's time to make some adjustments to your system. List-making and organization require some discipline, especially at first, but the payoff in stress reduction (and fewer trips to the tack seller at the show) is well worth it.

Timing is Everything

A friend once trotted by me in the warm-up and grimaced. "Don't you hate it when you've warmed up for six minutes too long?" she said. I do hate it, indeed! The best competitors are experts at using their time.

They know how much warm-up time their horse needs, how long it takes to ride to that warm-up area, how long it takes them to get dressed and tack up, and what time they need to load their horse on the trailer in order to be ready to go. Nothing is vague, and nothing is left to chance. Planning your schedule in detail allows you to show up at the right place, at the right time, with the right equipment, without a sense of hurry or frenzy.

Write. It. Down.

As with my stuff, I never trust my brain to keep track of my schedule. If I'm nervous at all (which only happens *every* time), my Lizard Brain starts losing and forgetting things. So I write *everything* down. I usually post my schedule on a white board or a piece of paper at my stall or the trailer, plus I put it in my phone so I have it with me anywhere on the show grounds. (Use an app that doesn't rely on cell service, just in case there is no coverage at the show—it does happen!) If you're the type of person who writes down a schedule but then forgets to look at it, set alarms on your phone as reminders.

If all of this sounds like what your mother told you about getting ready for school, you're right—and that's the point. Familiar systems help to soothe your Lizard Brain so that it doesn't get worked up about the small stuff, and that leaves your Rational Brain free to focus on the important things, such as memorizing your test or your jump course.

As always, remember to build some flexibility into your schedule. With horses, there's always something that doesn't go as planned: your horse rubs his braids out, your ring is running 30 minutes behind schedule, the truck has a flat on the way to the show. In other words, expect the unexpected! Build extra time into your schedule to cover your bases, and unexpected mishaps won't send your Lizard Brain into a frenzy.

The Day Before

I have a rule for myself: The day before I leave for an event, I don't practice my dressage test or school any of the difficult movements. This may seem counterintuitive, but it has to do with my perfection-driven personality. If I practice anything the day before, I end up drilling my horse and getting stressed about any movements that aren't up to my standards. It makes both of us miserable, so I don't let myself do it anymore. I usually go for a hack, or if it's raining, I'll do some really easy stretching work in the indoor.

It's critical to make the shift from training to performing in the days before a show. At this point, you are as prepared as you can possibly be, and you aren't going to teach your horse anything new in those last few days. We aim for constant improvement in our day to day training program, but competition is all about showing off your strengths and camouflaging your weak spots. Just as runners taper their workouts in the week before a marathon, plan to use your last week to polish what you've got. Do things that you can praise your horse for, so that he goes to the show feeling like the next Olympic candidate. Avoid confrontations or stressful situations with him. Giving him a positive week will leave him fresh and ready to give you his best when you arrive at the competition.

As always, the specifics of those last few days are unique to each individual horse and rider. Your horse may do well with very little work, while someone else's needs a full week of exercise to keep the edge off at the show. Notice what seems to work for you and your horse, and come up with your own routine for handling the countdown to show day.

On with the Show

You've arrived at the show, you've settled in, and it's time to get ready for your first class. You're as prepared as you can possibly be. How do you go in there and lay down your best performance?

Put It On

There's a great scene from the movie *Men In Black,* when Zed (Rip Torn) tells former cop and soon-to-be Agent J (Will Smith) to "put it on." When J asks, "Put what on?" Zed answers, "The last suit you'll ever wear." A few minutes later, Agent J emerges, all traces of his former life erased by that suit (and a killer pair of Ray Bans). He *is* one of the Men in Black.

So now it's time to "put it on." First: put on your Performance Self (p. 75). Picture stepping away from your Real Self and into your Performance Self. I like to do this when I change into my show clothes. Dirty t-shirt and jeans off: bye-bye Real Self, I'll be back later. Clean breeches, shiny boots, jacket, helmet on: Performance Self is here. Notice your posture: is it a Performance Self stance? Head high, eyes up, chest open, shoulders back, arms relaxed. If you are having a hard time finding it, channel your favorite rider—keep a photo of him or her handy in case you need a reminder. Does music get you into Performance Self mode? Now's the time to play that theme song!

Strike a Pose

Another way to put on Performance Self is by Power Posing. Warning: this is one of those things that's going to sound completely stupid. Try it anyway, because there is strong research evidence that it works. Find a private space somewhere, and for two minutes, put on a Superhero Power Pose: stand with your hands on your hips and your feet apart, like Wonder Woman or Superman. The other Power Pose is the Victory Pose: stand, again with feet apart, and your hands over your head in a V, as if you've just crossed the finish line and won a race.

These poses decrease stress hormones and increase feelings of power in the body. They will feel weird at first, but keep at it, because this is one situation where "Fake it till you make it" has been proven true. (Google "Amy Cuddy body language TED Talk" for a fascinating explanation of this. It is literally life-changing.) It only takes two minutes, and you can do it in the back of your trailer or even the porta-potty!

Tend to the Lizard

Now that you're in Performance Self, reassure your Lizard Brain. "It's okay, I've got this. We're ready to get out there; we're as prepared as we can possibly be." Review your plan with your Lizard Brain, so it knows you're on top of the situation, and you're not going headfirst into life-threatening danger. If your Lizard protests, Delete any negative thoughts or images it throws at you, and repeat your reassurances. This is not the time for discussions, it's time to get it done.

Find Your Focused Calm

Put all of your focus on the class at hand, and let go of any other rides you have coming up. Delete any thoughts that are unrelated to the current ride; those are Real Self concerns at the moment. Ride one class at a time, one moment at a time. Everything else stays with Real Self to deal with later, or gets Deleted if it's not helpful to your riding.

Every performance has weak links, areas that aren't quite up to your standards. The job of your Performance Self is not to make those weak links better; its job is to camouflage them as much as possible. Now is NOT the time to try for a huge trot lengthening if your horse can't do it in practice without breaking into canter. Let go of perfection, get through the tough parts as gracefully as possible, and show off your strong points. The best riders make mistakes all the time; they're just experts at making it *look* seamless.

Choose Your Mantra

Finally, find your Two-Beat Mantra for the class. Use soft images if your Lizard (or your horse's Lizard) is on overdrive, or use "fighting words" if you need to go out there in attack mode. Either way, take three or four soup breaths to get you into your Focused Calm mindset, and off you go! Any time your mind wanders or gets caught up in negative thinking, just hit Delete and bring it back to the present moment. You may have to do this multiple times, and that's fine; the more you practice, the easier this will get.

Take a Breath

Once you're riding, your Lizard Brain may still try to grab the reins. This usually happens in one of two ways. Some people go completely blank, forgetting their course or test, making mistakes they never make at home, such as cantering around on the wrong lead. Other riders go into fast-forward, rushing through their ride at a breakneck pace, while their horse is wondering where the tiger is. You can almost hear the Lizard shouting, "Quick! Let's get this over with so we can get out of here!" Unless you're a barrel racer or a jockey, this reaction is no help whatsoever. How can you stay present and keep your Rational Brain in charge, so you can do what you know how to do?

First, you need to...drum roll...wait for it...breathe. You're probably rolling your eyes again, but I'm willing to bet that if the Lizard is holding the reins, you're holding your breath or breathing too fast and too shallowly. Take a big, slow, soup breath, and then take another one. Really feel the breath going in and out, and notice whether your horse is breathing as well. He will often take a big breath when he feels us do so, and that's going to help quiet his Lizard Brain, too.

Do the Next Right Thing

Now, identify the first thing you need to do, and do it. Ride down the center line and halt, do your opening circle. As you do the first thing, identify the second thing: find your spot on the rail, track left, go to your first fence. Beginning is usually the hardest part; once you've begun, your rehearsals and practice will kick in, and you'll remember what to do next.

If you're still struggling for focus, or if your horse is tense and distracted, concentrate on the rhythm of your horse's stride. Focus on an even two-beat trot, a steady three-beat canter or lope. Good rhythm improves everything else, so it's an excellent place to put your attention when you feel scattered.

If something goes wrong—you get the wrong canter lead, or your horse bucks in the middle of a transition—*stay in the present moment*, and let the mistake go. Remember, ride the horse you have now, not

COLLEEN'S STORY: **WHEN THE WORST-CASE SCENARIO ACTUALLY HAPPENS**

Colleen planned to attend a local show over the weekend, and she had prepared everything down to the last detail, from packing the trailer to deciding exactly when she needed to leave the barn and arrive at the show.

Unfortunately, fate had other ideas: she got a flat tire on her way to the show grounds. She couldn't get the lug nuts loosened by herself, so she had to call someone to come and help her change the tire. By the time she got to the show grounds, she was an hour late, and by the time she had tacked up her horse, she had only five minutes to warm up her horse instead of the 30 minutes she had planned on.

Since she couldn't possibly do as much as she wanted to do, she decided the next right thing would be to get her horse into his slow, rhythmic jog. She knew that if she could get him to jog quietly, she could manage a decent lope in the class. She got him to jog quietly, and into her class she went. It wasn't the performance she had hoped for, but she managed to produce a decent ride by focusing on one right thing.

the horse you had two seconds ago. You can't fix the past, you can only ride in the present moment. Delete the mistake, and get going! Delete any thought that doesn't help you improve the situation. "I just blew it, there goes my qualifying score," does nothing to get you back on the correct lead. Thinking about the rail you just hit uses up valuable strides that you could be using to set up for the next jump. The sooner you recover your Focused Calm, the better chance you have of saving the rest of the performance.

All of this may sound deceptively simple, but that's exactly the point. Your mind needs to be free of clutter in order to produce your best performance. The fewer thoughts you have bouncing around, the more you will be able to focus on the feel of your horse and the quality of your ride.

The In-Between

If you are riding in more than one class or phase, chances are good that you will have some chunks of down time. It's essential that you remove your Performance Self for some of this time. Performance Self demands a huge amount of energy and focus, so you need to give your mind a break.

It's easy to use down time to rehash and analyze your last ride, or think about how you are going to handle your next one. That's fine up to a point, but it's easy to make yourself crazy with too many "if only's" or "what if's." Plan to have some distractions available. Listen to music, socialize with the riders around you, read a magazine. There is always tack to clean, a stall to pick out, or an aisle to sweep. Playing games on your phone or posting photos on Facebook or Instagram are great ways to kill some time as well.

Distress Tolerance

While coaching at an event recently, I had numerous people ask me for help in coping with their nerves. All of them were struggling with the "in-between time," when they had nothing to do and plenty to think about and obsess over. All of them also had fallen for two mistaken beliefs: One, they believed that if they just talked enough about their feelings, the bad feelings would go away. Two, they believed that those bad feelings had to go away in order for them to be okay.

"Distress Tolerance" is a phrase psychologists use for being able to stand it when we feel bad. The military has an even better phrase: "Embrace the suck." Sometimes you can't feel better right away, no matter what you do, so you need to get used to embracing the suck.

"But this is supposed to be fun," I heard repeatedly when I suggested this. Well, yes, showing is fun, but not in a pleasurable, go-to-the-beach kind of way. Competition is "fun" in an adrenaline-charged, feel-fulfilled-by-meeting-a-challenge kind of way. Tension, doubt, and uncertainty are all built into the experience. You can fight those emotions, which will make you feel worse, or you can embrace the suck and simply accept them. You don't have to *feel* okay to *be* okay. Acceptance allows you to get comfortable with being uncomfortable, and it makes you tougher, more resilient, and more flexible mentally. You'll still feel whatever you feel—jittery, edgy, anxious—but it will bother you a whole lot less.

It bears repeating: you do not have to *feel* okay to *be* okay. A woman I know gets extremely nauseated before her classes, to the point of getting dry heaves. "I've done it since I was a kid, and nothing I do changes it," she told me, "so I just don't let it bother me anymore." She is far from comfortable, but she is also just fine. She has learned to embrace the suck, and she knows it will go away once she gets to ride.

Leave the Escape Door Open

One last piece of advice before you go out there, and it may shock you: Give yourself permission to quit.

People freak out when I say this; apparently it's the most controversial idea I've come up with so far, because the pushback I get from it is intense. "If I give myself permission to quit, I'll do it every time—I'll go home and bake cookies and eat the whole batch. I'll let myself down, I know it."

MY STORY: **IT'S OKAY TO GO HOME**

As usual, I realized the need for an escape door through personal experience. I woke up at 4:00 am on the morning of my most challenging competition to date, one that had taken an entire year of careful preparation. My Lizard Brain was having a raging panic attack. "What are we doing? We can't do this. We're not ready. Those jumps are huge. That dressage test is impossible. The whole division is Olympic riders." It wasn't. But this was my Lizard talking. "We MUST. GO. HOME. NOW."

Suddenly, a small, quiet voice replied, "Then go home. It's okay. You don't have to do this. You can just tell people that your horse had some heat in his leg; no one will criticize you for looking after his best interests. You really don't have to do this."

I realized that the voice was right: I didn't *have* to do this. I could go home if I really needed to. No one was relying on me to deliver the cure for cancer that day; it was just another horse show.

All of a sudden, a huge weight lifted off my chest, and in the same moment, my Rational Brain and Lizard Brain both said at the same time: "Are you NUTS? Of COURSE we're going to do this! We've prepared all year! We can DO this!"

I doubt it, actually. People give themselves far too little credit; riders completely underestimate their own toughness. If you leave an escape door open, I guarantee you will almost never need to take it.

Here's the thing: flight animals hate to be trapped. A horse cast in a stall can kill himself flailing around, trying to escape. Your Lizard Brain is exactly the same way: it panics when it feels trapped. If you give it permission to quit, if it has an out, it doesn't need to panic. If your Lizard Brain doesn't need to panic, your Rational Brain can decide whether it's really a good idea not to ride today or if your Lizard Brain is just stressing out about the competition.

By offering your Lizard Brain an escape route, you allow it to feel safe, so it calms down, and your Rational Brain can remind it of what it already knows: that you *are* ready, and you *want* to do this. If you force it, your Lizard Brain will continue to panic and interfere with what you need to do to get through the challenge. And, on the off chance that your Lizard Brain is right and you aren't truly prepared, you give it a chance to have its say and consider your options.

Leave the escape door open, and you'll only use it when you really do need it.

THE AFTERMATH

When your ride is over, take a breath and give your horse a pat, no matter what happened out there. When you evaluate your performance, notice what went well and what needs work. It's easy to focus on the negative, especially if you didn't get a ribbon, but that is unfair to you and to your horse. Celebrate and give yourself credit for the positives, and remember that the negatives are simply indicators of what you need to work on; they aren't a statement about who you are as a rider or as a person. Even on the worst day, remind yourself that you Showed Up and put yourself out there. And if you had a great ride, let yourself bask in the warmth of that amazing feeling for a while!

Decompression Time

We have a post-show ritual at our farm: we always stop for ice cream on the way home. It's Celebration Ice Cream for everyone who had a good show, and Consolation Ice Cream for anyone who had a rough weekend. It's a chance for everyone to decompress, celebrate, support each other, and let go of any lingering stress or tension. (I'm sure our families appreciate that last part when the weekend hasn't gone as hoped!)

Give yourself time to wind down after the show, especially if you've had a rough weekend. Play the radio loudly, eat ice cream, vent to your fellow riders—anything that helps you settle down and get ready to re-enter your life in the Real World.

Don't Let Your Lizard Rewrite Your Plans

Be careful about making any major decisions or big changes to your training plan in the day or so after a show. Strong emotion, whether good or bad, lends itself to faulty judgment. If you're tempted on the drive home to sell your horse, fire your trainer, or move up to the next level, WAIT. Give yourself a day or two to settle, and then take a look at your next steps. You'll be glad you gave your Rational Brain a chance to catch up with your Lizard Brain, instead of letting the Lizard run amok!

 Riding Exercise: Practice for Show Situations

While it is impossible to recreate the exact energy and intensity of a show when you are at home, here are some exercises to help you practice coping with the competition environment.

1 Who Moved the Furniture?

Teach your horse to expect the unexpected. Place some objects around your riding area, such as lawn chairs, cones, or an old backpack, and move them around every couple of days. Practice keeping your horse's attention when she says, "Hey! That wasn't there yesterday!" Once you've mastered static objects, move on to noisy or flapping things. Empty grain bags, tarps, and plastic whirligigs are great for this.

2 Busy Warm-Up Arena
Get together with a few friends and ride as a group in a ring or small paddock—the smaller the area, the better. Practice staying focused on your ride as you work around each other. Work on claiming your space by keeping your eyes focused on where you are going, rather than trying to guess where the other person is going to go.

3 Crazy Warm-Up Rider
As above, but have one person designated to be "that rider" in the warm-up. That person can talk incessantly to her horse, cut people off, stop abruptly on the rail and talk on her cell phone, or any other frustrating behavior you can think of. Everyone else practices regaining focus after she disrupts their ride.

4 Practice Deleting Mistakes
Ride a test, pattern, or course, and say "Delete" out loud whenever you make a mistake in the pattern or if your riding isn't what you'd like it to be.

5 Lose Your Way
Ride a pattern as above, and have a friend blow a whistle at some random moment, as if you'd gone off course. Practice pausing, deleting any negative thoughts, taking a breath, identifying your next movement, and resuming your ride. Even if going off course means elimination in your particular discipline, practice resuming the ride anyway—it will improve your pattern-memorization skills.

6 Made You Look!
Ride in an imaginary class, and have people cause various distractions: shout your name, let a dog into the ring, open an umbrella, make catty comments about your riding as you go by.

Practice staying in Performance Self and keeping your horse focused on his work. Notice which distractions you are most vulnerable to, and practice these a lot.

7 Quick Reflexes

Ride a course, a pattern, or a test, but you don't get to learn it beforehand—have a friend call it out to you, one jump or one movement at a time. If you make a mistake, stop, breathe, and pick up where you went off course.

I'll leave you with one of my favorite quotes; I discovered it in a book by Brene Brown (see the list of References on p. 209), and it's from a speech by Teddy Roosevelt. It has come to be known as "The Man In the Arena," and it sums up perfectly for me what competition is all about, at the tiniest local show all the way up to the Olympics.

"It is not the critic who counts; not the man who points out how the strong man stumbles, or where the doer of deeds could have done them better. The credit belongs to the man who is actually in the arena, whose face is marred by dust and sweat and blood; who strives valiantly; who errs, who comes short again and again, because there is no effort without error and shortcoming; but who does actually strive to do the deeds; who knows great enthusiasms, the great devotions; who spends himself in a worthy cause; who at the best knows in the end the triumph of high achievement, and who at the worst, if he fails, at least fails while daring greatly, so that his place shall never be with those cold and timid souls who neither know victory nor defeat."

PART III

Battling the Big Demons

Beyond Stressful:
I Just Can't Get Over It

Me: *"When I was a kid and crashed from my horse,
I got back on and never gave it a second thought. Now, if I fall off,
I'm nervous about getting back on. It's so stupid!"*

Eric: *"Actually, normal people call that 'wisdom.'"*
—Actual conversation with my husband, 2014

The above exchange between my husband and me took place after I'd taken a tumble at a horse trials. I was fine, luckily, but it was a reminder that neither my body nor my mind bounce back the way they did when I was 12 years old. Eric's comment got me thinking that maybe my caution isn't such a bad thing after all; maybe I need to respect the reality that I'm not 12, and listen to the wiser part of my brain that wants me alive at the end of the day. This train of thought, however, seriously pisses me off. I *like* being tough, dusting myself off and getting right back on. I resent losing my ability to bounce.

It's a point of pride for most riders that we're tough enough to go right back to what we were doing as soon as medically possible. But sometimes, the Lizard Brain has other ideas, other needs. Sometimes an accident is traumatic enough that no matter how much we want to, we can't pick up where we left off, even if our physical injuries have healed. Sometimes we can't Just Get Over It.

This chapter covers what to do when you've had The Big One—a major fall, a serious injury (or injuries), or any experience that has scared you to the point that you can't just get back on and go back to where you left off. I'll talk about why some accidents are different from others, help you understand the nature of psychological injury, and show you some tools to help you stage your comeback. If you haven't read chapter 1 about the Lizard Brain, please read it before you go on as it's essential for understanding this work.

THE BIG ONE

You've experienced a bad fall with your horse. Perhaps you were seriously injured, or came very close. The experience itself may have been terrifying, even if you didn't get hurt. In any case, this one is different— it's Big, and it's not going away. Your Lizard Brain refuses to back down; if anything, it's on overdrive, reacting to every little thing. All the reassurance and planning in the world aren't cutting it.

Your Lizard Brain is right: some falls are different from all the others. And if a Big One happens, the Lizard is going to do everything in its power to prevent it from ever happening again. Let's start with the most obvious Big One: you were seriously injured. Broken bones, severe pain, and especially head trauma are no joke to your Lizard Brain. The loss of control in such an accident sends the Lizard into a protective frenzy. It knows that death was a real possibility this time, not just an abstract fear, and it will go to any lengths necessary to prevent it from happening again.

Even if you weren't seriously hurt, the Lizard Brain sometimes kicks into overdrive anyway. Sometimes "what could have happened" is enough to do the trick. If you have had a major injury in the past, a scary near-miss can trigger the memory of previous pain strongly enough that the Lizard says, "Enough. We're done. I've had it with the whole horse thing."

SHARON'S STORY: **WHEN THE WORLD SHOUTS AT YOU**

Sharon came to me because she was having severe anxiety while riding her new horse. He had bolted recently, and she fell off when he swerved to avoid a barrel in the arena. While she was just a little sore the next day, she was extremely shaken by the fall, and she found herself unbearably anxious whenever she headed to the barn to ride.

"I don't understand it," she told me. "I've had falls that were much, much worse than that, and I always got back on again with no trouble. What's wrong with me?"

It turned out that what was "wrong" with Sharon was a pair of devastating losses in her life. She had purchased the new horse because her beloved old gelding had died the year before. He was Sharon's trusted companion for nearly 20 years before she had to put him down due to his advanced age.

In addition to the loss of her horse, Sharon's best friend had died recently after a long battle with cancer. The two of them had always ridden together every week; now Sharon felt a huge hole in her life where her friend had been.

By itself, Sharon's fall might have shaken her trust in her new horse a little bit. But in combination with the losses of two of her closest, most trusted friends, it became overwhelming. She felt as if the world was shouting at her, "You can't rely on anything anymore!" Once she could see how those losses affected her experience of her fall, she was able to come gradually to terms with it, and start to rebuild trust with her new horse.

Complicating Factors

Parenthood also makes the Lizard more sensitive. A fall that might have been no big deal in your child-free past can be much more traumatic once you have little ones relying on you (or nearly grown ones with big tuition payments).

Outside circumstances often play a part in your reaction to an accident. If you are already stressed at work, or you are having trouble with your significant other, you may react more strongly to a scary event than you normally would. Stress has a cumulative effect, so if your Rational Brain is already putting out other fires, your Lizard Brain may take over and try to shut down any other sources of stress. "No way are you getting back on that horse. We don't have any reserves to spare if he tries to buck you off again."

Psychological Injury Is a *Real* Injury

It is absolutely essential to recognize that when you experience something that threatens your well-being, you suffer psychological injury, just as much as physical injury. You can't see the wounds (though neuroscience is learning to detect them), but *they are there, and they are just as real.* If your horse came in from the pasture with a bowed tendon, you wouldn't throw a saddle on him the next day and tell him to toughen up! You would put him on stall rest, medicate him, and cold hose and wrap the leg every day until it healed completely. You might even seek out specialized treatment such as shock-wave or stem-cell therapy to help him get better. You'd bring him back into work slowly, and if he hit a setback, you'd take a step back in the recovery process and wait until he was ready to move forward again.

Trying to "tough" your way through traumatic psychological injury is like forcing your horse to run on a bowed tendon. You have an injury, and you need to treat it gently and correctly so that you can recover.

Crash Comparison: Don't Do It

"But I've had way worse happen in the past, and it never bothered me like this."

"So-and-so rode through the rest of the show after he broke three ribs. I'm just a wuss."

"Why can't I just be like her? Nothing ever scares her."

We hear a lot about other people's accidents in our little equestrian world, even more so since the advent of social media. It's easy to see someone else's apparently spectacular comeback and feel like you should be able to do the same. But comparing crashes is pointless at best, and detrimental to your recovery at worst. No two bowed tendons are alike, and no two falls are the same either.

Remember the Brain Trap in chapter 3, Comparing Your Insides to Other People's Outsides (p. 58)? The same idea applies here. Spectacular comebacks make great magazine articles, but they don't tell the whole story; there are always deep low points of physical and mental struggle, even if you don't hear about them. You never know someone else's whole story, and your journey is your own. Let go of the weight of comparing yourself to others—it takes time and energy away from the effort of your own recovery.

It also doesn't help to compare this accident to ones that you've had in the past. As I mentioned earlier, your current life circumstances have a strong influence on your reaction to stressful situations. While you may have been unfazed by breaking some ribs in the past, this has no bearing on how you will react when you break some bones now. Each situation is unique, and your response is unique as well. Your response to a frightening event says absolutely nothing about your courage, your strength, or your skill as a rider. Your feelings are what they are, and they make sense in the context of your experience. Let go of expecting yourself to be 100 percent tough 100 percent of the time.

STAGING A COMEBACK

"How long does this take?"

This is the most common question I hear from clients who are sidelined by anxiety. The frustrating, obnoxious truth is that it will take as long as it takes. There are too many variables to pin down a number of days or weeks. There is good news, though: you *can* recover. What may surprise you is that the quickest way to do it is by taking the smallest, easiest steps you possibly can.

Back to my bowed-tendon analogy. Once a tendon heals and the horse is cleared to return to work, you don't throw the saddle on; instead, you do five minutes of hand-walking. After you do that, you bump it up to 10 minutes for a week or so, then to 15, and so on. Only after several weeks of hand-walking do you start work under saddle. Rush the process, and you risk re-injury, possibly worse than the first time.

Serious injuries to your psyche need the same careful treatment as that recovering tendon. Move too quickly, try to do too much too soon, and you risk re-traumatizing yourself, possibly worse than the first time around. You need small, gentle, doable tasks every day to help you feel safe, yet challenged, so that you grow stronger without scaring yourself into a major setback.

Before your brain explodes from the sheer tedium that this process implies, let me point out that the bowed tendon analogy has its limits. You should give yourself the same care, patience, and compassion that you would give your horse if he were seriously injured. However, you're a human, not a horse, and your bigger Prefrontal Cortex and Rational Brain give you a major advantage here. The time frame and the level of challenge depend completely upon you and how you feel. There may be times when you feel you're progressing at a snail's pace, but there will be other times when you experience major breakthroughs that lead to surges in your confidence. Success breeds more success, and you may find that once you get a toehold into the recovery process, you'll move along quickly and your confidence will return.

Acknowledgment

In chapter 1, I pointed out that fear is your body's alarm system, a warning that there is danger afoot, and if you don't acknowledge that warning, the alarm will get louder until you do. This is especially true when an experience was truly dangerous or life-threatening. Bottle up your emotions about a traumatic experience, and they are guaranteed to leak out or finally explode all over you. In order to heal, you need to acknowledge your feelings about what happened.

This process won't be fun; it will probably hurt, and it often hurts a lot. You may find several layers of emotion once you scratch the surface. There's the fear about the memory and the possibility of it happening again, fear of the physical pain, fear of what others may think. You may feel guilty or responsible for what happened. You may also feel grief for the loss of trust you had in your horse, or even anger at his failure to take care of you. You may grieve for the person you once were, for the carefree attitude you had before your accident. After the fall I described in chapter 2 (p. 29), I had to grieve the loss of my fearlessness; that loss made me both sad and angry.

Sometimes the emotions will seem nonsensical—"Why would I expect my horse to take care of me when we were being chased by a huge dog?"—but it doesn't matter if they make logical sense. Allow yourself to feel them anyway. Emotions don't exist on the same plane as logic, but they are just as real and just as important. Once you let them happen, they can run their course and move on. Some emotions will come up many times, but each time you acknowledge them and allow yourself to feel them, you will have worked through another layer and taken another step toward recovery.

Exercise: Give the Lizard Some Air Time

(Note: Do this exercise when you have at least 30 minutes to yourself to allow any strong feelings to run their course before you have to go do other adult-ish things, like make dinner or drive somewhere.)

On a piece of paper (or six), write down every thought and feeling you have about what happened to you. Don't censor or worry whether it makes sense—just write, and let the Lizard have its say. It may be painful at first, but it can't actually hurt you, and it will feel better as you move forward.

When you finish, thank your Lizard for working so hard to protect you from further danger. Let it know that you're going to take your recovery one step at a time, and you won't let it get overwhelmed. Remind it that you survived even this scary experience, and reassure it that you are going to do everything you can to be safe while moving forward.

Elizabeth Gilbert, author of *Eat, Pray, Love*, has a wonderful description of how she handles fear. She tells her fear that they're going on a road trip (for her, that trip is writing a new book; for our purposes, it's getting back to riding again). Fear is invited to come along on the trip, because it's a part of her and she loves and accepts all the parts of her. However, Fear isn't allowed to drive, to choose the destination, or choose the music on the radio. As you embark on your recovery, remember that your Lizard may whine a bit and need to stop and go to the bathroom a lot, but it's not allowed to choose the day's activity or to hold the reins.

Take Small Bites and Chew Slowly

"When eating an elephant, take one bite at a time."
—Army General Creighton Abrams

Okay, so the idea of eating an elephant is pretty gross. But you get the picture: the easiest way to do anything hard is to do one small piece of it, then another piece, then another. Getting over your experience and back to riding will involve a series of steps, sometimes so small they may feel meaningless or ridiculous at the time—but they *will* get you there. In fact, the smaller each step feels, the better. When you accomplish something small, your skittish Lizard exhales and says, "Hey, that was easy. This next thing probably won't be so bad either. I can stay over here, out of the way, since it doesn't look like we're going to die anytime soon." If a step feels too big and threatening, though, your Lizard will morph into a giant Komodo Dragon and chase you as far back into your comfort zone as you can possibly go. So, here we go—one easy step at a time.

Exercise: The Comeback Plan

It's time to write out a comeback plan. Put your goal at the top, and then write down every step you can think of between where you are now and where you want to go. See Sarah's Story (p. 144) as an example.

Everyone's plan will look different, but every plan should have many steps—when it doesn't, you're trying to bite off too much of the elephant at once. You can always take another small bite if the first one goes down easily. Some days you may be able to check several steps off the list; other days, especially if you're stressed in other parts of your life, one step may be all you can handle. You may even find that you need to repeat a step several times, and that's just fine.

Often, people base their steps on what they could do before the accident happened. This usually backfires, because they haven't healed enough yet to move that quickly. It's essential to plan steps that feel easy for you *now*, not ones that you think you *should* be able to handle

SARAH'S STORY: **SMALL BITES**

Sarah took a nasty fall while cantering through a field with some friends. She broke two vertebrae in her neck, along with several ribs, and suffered a concussion. She has been medically cleared to ride, and she wants to get back to trail riding, but even the thought of getting on her horse makes her heart race and twists her stomach into knots. It's all she can do to get herself to the barn to groom her horse. Here is her recovery plan.

Sarah's goal: To go back to trail riding in a group and be able to canter confidently across that field again.

Steps to get there:

• Go to the barn every day and spend time brushing her horse and hanging out with her horse friends.
• Hand-walk her horse, both in the ring and outside.
• Sit on her horse in the ring with someone holding her.
• Have a "pony ride" in the arena with someone leading her.
• Get comfortable walking, trotting, and cantering in the arena (may actually be several separate steps).
• Ride her horse down the driveway at a walk.
• Go for a very short trail ride at the walk with someone she trusts.
• Trot outside the ring.
• Canter outside the ring.
• Walk through the field where she fell.
• Trot, then canter through the field where she fell.

easily. This will be frustrating a lot of the time. That's okay; be frustrated, get pissed off, cry, curse, whatever you need to do—then break the steps down into smaller ones.

When Sarah (see her story above) started to execute her plan, she got overwhelmed when it was time for a "pony ride" on her horse. Her

Lizard Brain was just too keyed up and couldn't trust that she would be safe, so it gave her a full-blown panic attack to keep her from getting on. She was frustrated, to put it mildly (there was a lot of language not fit to print here), but she scaled back and decided to do a pony ride on one of the barn's confirmed old schoolmasters first.

After this experience, when it came time for her to walk through the field where her accident had happened, she decided to add an extra step and go out to that field on foot first. This turned out to be an excellent idea, because when she got there for her walk, she became extremely emotional and was flooded with memories of the accident, which took her by surprise. The smaller step gave her time to cope with her feelings, and when it came time to ride through the field, things went relatively smoothly.

Zero to "10": Using the Anxiety Scale

How can you judge whether a step is the right size for you? Any action should stretch you just outside your current comfort zone. When you think of doing a particular action, notice how much anxiety you feel. On an Anxiety Scale of zero to "10," if zero equals "totally fine" and "10" equals "paralyzed with terror," how anxious are you? If your answer is between "4" and "6," it's a good step to do. Anything below "4" probably won't challenge you enough to grow your comfort zone, and anything above "6" can trigger your Fight or Flight Response to the point where you won't be able to think clearly or function effectively.

Your goal each time is not only to do a particular step, but to *keep doing it until your anxiety drops at least two points.* This reassures your Lizard Brain that you're fine, which increases your confidence and grows your comfort zone. Sarah had to be willing to be led around the arena on that schoolmaster as many times as it took for her to come down from a "6" to a "4."

What if you're at a "6," and your anxiety won't budge—or worse, it spikes to an "8"? Break it down even more. When the thought of being led around the arena on her own horse made Sarah's anxiety shoot up to a "9," she switched gears and they pulled out that schoolmaster. If he hadn't been available at that particular time, she could have just sat on her horse without moving until her anxiety decreased two points. If that were still too much, she could have gone back to leading her horse around for that day until she came down two points. She could have even asked someone else to lead him while she kept a hand on his body, until the sensation of his movement made her less anxious. The key here is to find something you *can* do that drops your anxiety by two points.

This will never be a completely linear process. You will probably find that on some days, something that only sent you to a "3" on the anxiety scale last week now shoots you up to a "6" or "7." This is frustrating, but it's completely normal, especially if you're stressed or tired on a given day. When this happens, go back and repeat an earlier step that keeps you between "4" and "6," and do it until your anxiety drops two points or more. It is much more effective to go back and repeat a step than to try to force progress when your Lizard Brain is having a bad day. Don't hassle yourself for this; recognize it as part of the healing process, accept it, and do what your Lizard Brain needs you to do. Often, you'll bounce back to the higher steps quickly after giving yourself a do-over like this.

Find a Steady Eddy

Let me stop here for a minute to sing the praises of schoolmasters. If your horse feels like too much to handle right now, or he is likely to repeat the behavior that got you into trouble in the first place, get some time on a horse that's bombproof. You can reassure yourself that you still know how to ride, and work on any weak spots without wondering whether you're going to end up on the ground all over again. Doing this also prevents an anxiety loop from forming between you and your horse—you're anxious, so he gets anxious, so you get more anxious, and so on.

Discretion Is Often the Better Part of Valor

Similarly, don't hesitate to ask someone else to deal with a behavior problem in your horse. If you got hurt because your horse's spin-and-bolt maneuver put you on the floor, you may not be the right person to fix that problem. You understandably are defensive and protective of your body after you have been injured, but those are not useful attitudes when we need to correct a behavior problem.

In addition, your horse may have been upset or even traumatized by what happened, and he may need some time to regain his own confidence. This can be a lot easier with a rider who isn't bringing any baggage to the situation. You will regain your confidence and trust in your horse much more quickly if you know that both you *and* your horse have made progress. This may be hard to swallow if you are used to doing your own training and solving your horse's problems, but a bruised ego heals quickly—ask me how I know!

"It's a Learning Experience" and Other Annoying Platitudes

This whole process, in fact, will probably be humbling on a lot of levels, especially if you're accustomed to forging fearlessly ahead and handling things on your own. In the Addiction and Recovery community, this is known as an AFGO—Another F***ing Growth Opportunity! You may eventually look back on it and realize it made you a better rider and even a better person, but in the thick of it, it's just really, really hard sometimes. It may mean a change in how you see yourself as a rider, and maybe even how you see yourself as a person. As I mentioned earlier, you may find yourself grieving for your old self, the one who used to just get back on and keep going. The loss of that self can be painful, and it's also completely normal. It's the way that our brains teach us to learn from our mistakes and make us less likely to get hurt again.

Please, above all else, give yourself the same care and kindness during this process that you would give your horse. If he were in a terrible trailer accident, would you be angry if he didn't want to get right back on a trailer afterward? Would you call him a chicken if he were reluctant to jump after crashing through a fence? Of course not—you would help him along, one step at a time, until he regained his confidence. Please, do the same for yourself—you deserve it, and anything else will make things worse instead of better.

Other People

There are other people involved in this recovery process as well, people who have their own feelings and reactions about what happened. Family members may have been deeply affected, and they may be understandably fearful of your return to riding. It's important to take the time to talk about what happened and to acknowledge that our loved ones have been through a lot also.

Especially when they aren't horse people, they may demand that you stop riding, sell your horse, or even have it put down. Instead of reacting by hurling your own ultimatums—"You can't keep me from riding, I'll choose my horse over you!"—try to see that these demands are a response to their fear that something even worse could happen next time. Remember, their Lizard Brain is probably shouting at them that they'll die if they lose you. They need their fears and pain acknowledged, too. Try to find a time to discuss it when emotions aren't running so high, and work toward a recovery plan that both of you can accept. This conversation will probably need to happen repeatedly as the process moves forward, and as you come to terms with what your future with horses will look like.

Unwelcome Feedback

Well-meaning friends, coworkers, and even health-care professionals may offer their opinions on your situation, solicited or otherwise. Many of these will be some variation on "Are you insane? You are going to try

KATE'S STORY: **SCALING DOWN**

Kate, a polo player in her early forties, took a nasty fall a couple of years ago, one that required back surgery to correct. When she started riding again, her husband insisted that she needed to give up polo for good. He could handle her riding, but the polo matches had to go. Kate was equally insistent that she would give *him* up before she gave up playing polo! Their marriage was taking a serious beating from all of the arguing.

Finally, one day Kate's husband broke down and said, through tears, "I just couldn't stand it if something happened to you again. It really hit home this time that I could actually lose you, and that thought was more than I could take."

Kate hadn't realized just how frightening the fall had been to her husband; now that she saw the real pain and fear he was experiencing, she understood that he wasn't just being overprotective. On the other hand, she really wasn't ready to give up polo completely.

They eventually found a compromise: Kate would start with just going to practices, on the steadiest, calmest horse in the barn. She would work up to playing in matches again gradually, and only when her coach said there was no question that she was ready. It was a level of scaling down that Kate could accept, and a level of risk that her husband could tolerate. They agreed to talk about it again if any problems arose, such as complications from her back surgery.

this again?" Christopher Reeve will undoubtedly be mentioned, if his name hasn't already been invoked. You will probably get plenty of unsolicited advice, as well as be subjected to others' stories of their own or their acquaintances' trauma, riding-related or otherwise. It's a little like the way people touch a pregnant woman's belly: all of a sudden, social boundaries disappear, and people say or do things they would never say or do in normal circumstances.

This outside commentary can feel like an ambush, especially when you're already struggling with powerful and complicated feelings of your own. It can help to have a few prepackaged responses ready. Which one you use depends on the person. I like to divide advice-givers into three categories:

1 Stakeholders: people who are most important to me, including my family, my close friends, my trainer, and my doctor.

2 Concerned Supporters: friends and people who genuinely care about me, but generally aren't directly involved, and usually don't know much about horses.

3 Onlookers: people who know nothing about riding and whose opinions don't really matter to me, but who insist on putting in their two cents anyhow.

For *Stakeholders*, I only use a rehearsed response when I'm not ready to talk about the situation. My response is usually something along these lines: "I know what happened was scary for you. It scared me too, and I promise I'm being careful and thoughtful. Let's talk some more about this later."

For *Concerned Supporters*: "Thanks for your thoughts. I appreciate that I've got a good group of people looking out for me as I get back on track."

For *Onlookers*: "That's an interesting perspective. I'll keep it in mind."

You can always go into more detail if you want to, but if you don't, the canned responses usually let people know that you don't want to discuss it further. I use the shortest, least informative responses with the Onlookers. They usually don't know what they're talking about, and their opinions don't matter to me—they don't have any skin in the game.

Coping with Permanent Change

Full recovery is not always possible. Some physical injuries result in permanent disability. As I write this, one of eventing's brightest stars is entering his fourth week in the hospital due to a traumatic brain injury. Odds are, his high-performance days are over. Some injuries may not mean the end of riding, but require a scaling down of intensity or risk. Other injuries are more psychological in nature, leaving you feeling that you don't want to return to riding at all, or to a particular discipline, or to a particular horse.

Whatever form it takes, permanent change nearly always means a sense of loss, and loss leads to grief. It's very tempting to skip over this complicated emotional experience. It's so much easier to say, "Well, it is what it is. Everything happens for a reason, and I just have to accept it." Friends and family might even be relieved if you jump to this faux-acceptance. After all, a loved one's grief makes us feel sad, and very often powerless. You will probably get a lot of praise and encouragement for your positive, brave, bootstrapping attitude. We Americans love the can't-get-me-down outlook, and it makes for much better social media posts. Grief, on the other hand, is messy, awkward, painful, and hard for everyone involved.

Feel it anyway.

I'm not suggesting that you break down sobbing in a board meeting, or that crying itself is the only appropriate expression of grief. I'm saying that it's critical to be honest about your feelings, first to yourself, and then to the Stakeholders in your life. Allow your emotions to be whatever they are, instead of rushing past them to get some kind of "closure." Allow them to be messy and complicated, if that's what they are (and at some point, they probably will be). Trust that where you are now is not where you always will be. As with fear and anxiety, the way out of grief is straight through the middle, and it takes as long as it takes.

WHEN YOU JUST CAN'T GET OVER IT

Sometimes, a frightening experience doesn't get less frightening with time—it gets worse. The Lizard Brain's switch seems to get stuck, leading to a feeling of Fight or Flight all the time. Or that switch may go on the fritz, switching between intense hyperarousal and a sense of deadness or numbness. The incident may replay itself over and over in your mind, interrupting your other thoughts. You may have nightmares about it. You may have flashbacks, which are feelings that the event is recurring right now, in this moment. Depression and irritability, feeling cut off from other people, trouble sleeping and concentrating, and avoiding things that remind you of the event are also indicators that the Lizard Brain is in overdrive. If any of this sounds familiar, you may be experiencing Post-Traumatic Stress Disorder, or PTSD.

One of my clients was floored when I suggested she might have PTSD. "Isn't that what happens to soldiers who have been in combat? What happened to me was nothing like that." Combat, however, is only one situation that can trigger PTSD. Any exposure to actual or threatened serious injury or death can activate the symptoms.

A full discussion of PTSD is beyond the scope of this book; however, as a former trauma therapist, I can attest that people can and do get better with treatment. A good therapist who understands trauma can help you through the process of recovery. Even if you don't think you have PTSD, I strongly encourage you to seek therapeutic support if you are having intrusive memories or flashbacks, overwhelming surges of emotion, difficulty sleeping, frequent interpersonal conflicts, or trouble getting through your normal daily routines. It isn't necessary for the person you work with to understand horses—you can fill in their knowledge gaps there. The most important factors are that the therapist has experience treating traumatic experiences, and that you feel safe and comfortable with her or him.

Whatever your situation, if you still want horses in your life in some capacity, it is always possible. You may switch disciplines, or continue in the same area but at a less intense level. Para-equestrian programs are thriving in the United States and other parts of the world, as are therapeutic riding programs. If you can't ride but can handle a horse safely on the ground, you might even make a great volunteer for these programs. Honor your past riding identity, but stay open to new possibilities. Horses welcome us, whether we come to them in boots and spurs or in a wheelchair.

The Right Horse
Brings Less Stress

"If this horse were my boyfriend, I'd be in an abusive relationship."

"He's really good most of the time. He only rears when it's windy outside."

"I know I'm a beginner and my horse is green, but we can learn together."

"Well, yes, he bucked me off yesterday. Yeah, he bit me again. Oh, you heard about that? Yes, he did charge me when I went into his stall. But I love him!"

"I just know he'd be the perfect horse for me if he would just let me get on him."

I have heard every single one of these lines at one time or another. When I hear them, my heart sinks a little, because I know there's a rough road ahead, no matter what the end result turns out to be.

OPENING PANDORA'S BOX

I did *not*—repeat, *did not*—want to write this chapter. And by did not want to, I mean I would rather eat beets every day for a year while being forced to listen to *Wonderful Tonight* played on eternal repeat. Every trainer I know absolutely dreads having to approach the issue of whether their student is on the wrong horse, and many avoid it for as long as humanly possible. We know we're in for a rocky ride at best, and getting fired at worst, if we dare to broach this topic with a student.

The reason that trainers hate and fear talking to students about this is because as riders, students and trainers alike, we are all deeply attached to our horses; that emotional connection is a major reason why we own them. Trainers know that just asking the question, "Is this the right horse for you?" can open Pandora's Box. Many riders spend multiple years and multiple thousands of dollars trying to mold themselves and their horse into the perfect match. No one wants to lift the lid on the box, for fear of the torrent of emotions and implications that may be unleashed.

I obviously decided to write the chapter. (There might have been just a teensy bit of pressure from a few colleagues who were avoiding Pandora's Boxes in their own barns.) Once I thought about it, I realized that this book is a great place for this conversation, really. For one thing, I have experience from both sides of the fence: I've had to accept that I was riding the wrong horse, and I've had to tell my students that theirs isn't right for them. Also, this book is a low-stakes, safe location. You and I don't have to look each other in the eye when we talk about this; you can think about these ideas for as long as you want, get upset about them if you need to, and you can just stop reading if you get really irritated.

A book won't say "I told you so," and it has no skin in the game of Should He Stay or Should He Go. I won't try to convince you what kind of horse you should get, or to get rid of the horse you have, or to get a new one. If you are considering a new horse purchase, this chapter will help you ask yourself some important questions that will increase the odds of finding a great match. If you are questioning your relationship with your current horse, I hope to offer some thoughts and observations, and to help you look at your current situation from a fresh perspective.

First of all, how do you find the right horse for you? It's a little bit like finding a new boyfriend or girlfriend, really: you're attracted to someone, you "try them out" on a couple of dates, and then you consider whether you want to commit. You usually have some criteria in mind beforehand, and you compare those criteria to the actual individual once you meet him or her.

Since both dating and horse shopping in the twenty-first century usually begin online, let's imagine what your online ad would look like for the perfect horse.

Your Equine Personal Ad
Warning: cheesy exercise ahead. Feel free to roll your eyes and groan as much as you want, but I encourage you to give it a shot. And it can be kind of fun.

Imagine you are on the human-equine equivalent of Cupid.com, and you're going to take the plunge to write your "in search of" personal ad. First, write a profile of yourself as a rider: what types of riding you love, your strongest personality traits, your body type, your experiences, what you're hoping to accomplish. Unlike a humans-only online dating site, you can be completely honest here, because you don't have to worry about impressing the horse. If you're not sure how to describe yourself, ask a friend or trainer you trust how they would describe you.

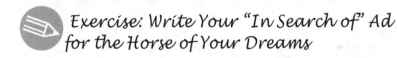 *Exercise: Write Your "In Search of" Ad for the Horse of Your Dreams*

1 Write a profile of yourself as a rider (in as much detail as possible). Include your body type, age, lifestyle details (for example, kids or no kids, full-time job or plenty of leisure time), activities you enjoy and the ones you don't, a description of your skills and personality as a rider, and anything else you feel is important.

2 Now, the fun part: write your "in search of" ad for the horse of your dreams. Include everything you can think of that you want in your perfect equine partner. Tall, dark, and handsome, or small, catty, and quick? Big and strong, or long and lean? Mr. Right (I'll keep you forever!) or Mr. Right Now (I need you to teach me the next level of skill)? Do you prefer girls, boys, or both?

Be as descriptive as you can about the horse's personality: Laid back? Sensitive? Steady-Eddy? Loves speed, or loves long, slow ambles? Demanding or quick to forgive and forget? Gives you a thrill or a deep sense of security? Needs daily attention or just likes to hang out a couple of times a week? Likes kids or likes to bite them? Loves to be pampered or prefers to wallow in the mud? Snuggly or businesslike?

Try to come up with at least 10 descriptive words or phrases. Also, include any deal-breakers. "Must leap ditches without a second thought," is my Number 1 deal-breaker, and "No lazy bones need apply," is a close second.

TESLA'S STORY: **ISO SCOPEY CROSS**

Here's an ad written by my student, Tesla, when she was looking for a horse to move up to the upper levels:

"ISO competitive partner, age 8 to 14, 15.3 to 16.2 hands. Preferably full Thoroughbred, will consider a scopey cross with a lot of blood if he has a soft, ground-covering gallop. Ideally forward-thinking and responsive but with a sense of self-preservation. Must have competition experience through Preliminary or above, with the ability to take a joke or pick up the slack (to save my stupid butt). Not willing to put up with exuberant airs above the ground in warm-up. Does not have to be well schooled on the flat, but should have solid basics and quality gaits. Must be manageable on the ground. Pre-purchase exam required."

Once you've finished the ISO exercise, step back and take a look at the list, and rate each quality on a scale from "1" (nice to have, but not at all important) to "5" (absolutely critical). And be ruthlessly honest. If you really care that a horse is a flashy chestnut with four white socks, don't rate that quality a "1" just because your trainer keeps telling you that looks aren't important. No horse is perfect, so you'll have to compromise at some point about some of your priorities, but for now, go with your true feelings. This helps you clarify what's most important to you.

Height, for example, is about a "2" for me. I like my horses between 15.3 hands and 16.2 hands, but I'll take 15.1 if he's a great jumper or 17.1 if he's not as long as a cruise ship. Bravery, though, is a "5": I need my horse to go out there with a "no problem, I've got this" mentality.

As you review your list, do plenty of honest soul-searching. Ask yourself, "Why is this trait important to me? Does it suit who I am right now, or who I wish I were? Am I buying the same problem I've had in the past?" (We all go for a type; it helps to be honest about the "dark sides" we're attracted to.) "Do I tend to skip over a kind soul because I'm distracted by shiny things?" There are no right answers and no judgments here, just an honest exploration of what you really value in a partner. If you want a great athlete but also a pet you can snuggle with, you need to pass over the one who can jump the moon but whose barn nickname is The Troll.

Finish "creating" your ideal equine partner by rewriting your list with all of the "5" traits at the top, then the "4s," and so on. If you are horse shopping, you now have your priority list. If you're evaluating your current partner, this gives you some objective criteria to work with.

Evaluate Your Current Horse

If you already have a horse and are questioning whether you are a good match, you need to add one more profile to your Personal Ad: your current horse. Describe him with as many phrases as you can, just as you did when you described your "perfect" match. Now line up all three lists: your own profile, your ideal horse's qualities, and your own horse's profile. Assuming you've been really honest with all three lists, how well do they match up?

Unfortunately, I can't give you a formula—"Seven matches, keep him; five or less, sell him"—any more than I could for someone's marriage. There are just too many variables in a horse and rider relationship to treat it so simplistically. Some indicators, however, can point you in a particular direction.

GOOD TIMES: THE EXCEPTION OR THE RULE?

Every relationship has difficult and even painful periods. Usually, working through those periods brings resolution to the problems, and the partnership grows as a result. Frustration and confusion are common emotions in these situations, but they resolve as you work through the areas where you are stuck. Most of the time you can see the light at the end of the tunnel, or you can at least believe that it's there when everything seems dark.

Dead-end relationships are different. Good times are the exception, and frustration and confusion are the norm. You may feel persistent fear or even dread when you think about coming to ride. You might find yourself avoiding the barn, probably justifying it by how busy you are. Deciding more and more often not to "pick a fight" by addressing a problem behavior is an indicator that things aren't working.

"Nothing I Do Makes a Difference"

Another red flag is a sense of helplessness, that nothing you do makes a dent in the problem. Ironically, you may also find yourself getting angry and defensive with other people if they suggest that it's time to move on. Many people feel depressed and start to doubt their abilities as a rider. They wonder if they should have been able to see the problems coming, if it was obvious all along (even though usually it wasn't). All of these emotions and experiences point to the possibility that you and your horse have hit a dead end.

This realization can be gut-wrenching. The first time I experienced it, I locked myself in my horse's stall and melted down for a solid hour. Before that, I spent the better part of three years trying to avoid admitting it to myself. The horse was a lovely Dutch Warmblood mare, and the first horse I'd started from babyhood, so I was very attached to her. When she was good, we won; when she was bad, we got eliminated. It was good enough just often enough that I was convinced it must have been me; I thought I could fix it. Maybe if I tried this strategy, or rode with that trainer, or used a different vet, I would find the magic bullet. It was agonizing—for me, for my horse, and for the people who loved me and were watching me suffer.

It was my mentor, Denny Emerson, who finally laid me out flat with the reality of the situation. He pulled me aside after watching me get eliminated at a show yet again. "Andrea, you need a new event horse," he said, not unkindly. "This one is going to wreck your riding. You've done everything possible. She just doesn't want to play the game."

Even writing this, 13 years later, I still feel a little jab of pain and sadness. "Giving up" doesn't sit well with me, and I loved that horse deeply. When it was good, it was great—we won a lot of events together. But when it was bad, it was awful—really, truly awful. After I finished my meltdown and picked myself up from the floor of her stall, I still felt devastated, but I also felt a sense of relief and liberation; someone I respected had told me the truth, and I could see it clearly now. I was ready to move on.

"Moving on" can mean many things besides simply selling a horse. In this case, I switched my mare to straight dressage, which eventually

MACKENZIE'S STORY: "I LOVE HIM MORE"

MacKenzie, one of my first students, had a little pony that couldn't jump higher than 2'3", and she had progressed beyond this level. I told her that if she wanted to keep moving forward, she needed a new horse. After a few weeks, she came back to me and said, "Andrea, I love this horse more than I love riding. I'm not going to sell him." How could I argue? She happily continued to trail ride and jump little jumps with him, and she never regretted her decision—in fact, she still owns him, more than 10 years later. The bigger jumps will still be there for her if she ever changes her mind.

made a huge impact on the quality of my riding when I found my next event horse.

I did eventually sell that Dutch mare; I'm a jumper at heart, and I wanted her to be appreciated for who she was. All of us have to come to our own terms with that decision, and we can only do that when we are ready to see the true picture with no filters and no rationalizations.

EIGHT ODD COUPLES

Here are some common mismatches that I see (or have experienced myself) between horses and riders. Some feel like you've been accidentally miscast in a romantic comedy, while others are worthy of full horror-flick status. See if any of these feel vaguely, or not-so-vaguely, familiar.

1 He's Green—and so Are You

You have just started riding in the last couple of years, or you've taken it up again recently after riding a little bit in your childhood. You looked at a couple of schoolmaster types, but they were all older and needed a fair amount of maintenance. And they were, well, kind of plain. You found a gorgeous three year old that was as sweet as could be, and the seller said it was the easiest youngster they had ever worked with. You don't have the opportunity to take regular lessons, but you do ride in an occasional clinic, so you figured you could get some guidance there if you got stuck.

Unfortunately, though, it's not progressing as smoothly as you thought it would. The horse has started getting really pushy on the ground, and you're having a hard time controlling him under saddle. He has started to test you with misbehaviors here and there, and you're worried, because they seem to be escalating in their intensity.

Even "straightforward" young horses are a challenge if you have never trained your own horse before. They really are blank slates, and they don't know what you're asking for. If you know how to ride but you don't know how to develop a training system for a green horse, it's easy to confuse him; if you aren't 100 percent sure what to ask for and how to ask, he won't understand what he's supposed to do.

Green horses are also unpredictable by nature; they haven't developed an attention span or a work ethic yet, so they're easily distracted or spooked. Like toddlers who have just learned to walk, they can move incredibly fast in random directions, and get away from you quicker than you ever thought possible. And they're *strong.* Training a youngster can be deeply rewarding, but it can also go very wrong if you aren't sure how to go about it.

2 The Horse for the Rider You Wish You Were

You're 5'1" and just learning to sit the trot. Your ambition is to ride Grand Prix dressage someday. You wish you were tall and elegant with long legs, able to float along in perfect harmony with your equally elegant horse. Your trainer urged you to get a lovely 15.2-hand Welsh cross, but you were afraid you would look silly in the warm-up ring among all those big, gorgeous Warmbloods. You buy a 17.2-hand Hanoverian with an enormous trot. You can't sit to that trot, and his power feels kind of overwhelming, but he's so gorgeous....

Unfortunately, you're not going to be 5'10" someday, unless you're 12 years old at the moment. Yes, Carol Lavell was petite and her Olympic dressage champion, Gifted, was 17.3, but we remember that about them because they were the exception, not the rule. Having a horse that suits your body type, especially if you are first developing your seat, makes everything easier and much, much more fun.

The other mismatch here is in temperament: you choose an off-the-track Thoroughbred because you'd like to be a rider who loves speed, excitement, and flash. You're truly happiest when you ride your friend's horse that feels like a well-broken-in pair of jeans, but maybe this time you'll find true love with the Glamour Boy in the sports car....

If you're hard-wired to love security, the James Dean Thoroughbred will never do anything but scare you; if you crave speed and excitement, that Belgian draft cross is unlikely to do it for you, no matter how well he jumps. You are who you are, and as long as you are safe riding the horse that suits your personality, he's the one for you.

3 The Three-Years-from-Now Horse

This is the horse that many parents want for their kids, the one that's showing three or four levels above the kid's ability level, "One that they can grow into, so we don't have to keep buying and selling horses as she progresses."

You can buy a pair of boots for a child that are two sizes too big, and they will grow into them in short order, usually with no ill effects besides a blister or two. Horses, however, don't work this way. More advanced horses are usually more sensitive to the aids, so they do exactly what you tell them to do—whether you meant to tell them that or not. With a less experienced rider, one of two things is likely to happen with a much more advanced horse: 1) He will object strenuously to your lack of experience, or 2) he will eventually regress to your ability level.

I couldn't have ridden my current horse if it hadn't been for the Irish mare I'd had before I bought him. The mare was a "4" on a "1-to-5" scale of sensitivity, and he is definitely a "5"; what I learned from Bailey was essential before I was ready to handle Chauncy. A horse that challenges you at the edge of your ability can definitely improve your riding, but if he is too far above your current level, you may become overwhelmed, and your comfort zone will shrink rather than expand.

At this point you may be thinking, "Hey, Andrea, didn't you just rave in the last chapter about how great it is to have a schoolmaster?" Yes. And it is. The difference between a schoolmaster and the three-years-from-now horse is that a schoolmaster can take a joke. A schoolmaster has a "been there, done that" attitude, and tends to be unfazed when we blunder about, learning the ropes.

The three-years horse, on the other hand, takes it personally when we aren't up to scratch; he is more sensitive and picky about how he is ridden, which leads to him feeling annoyed and to us feeling over-mounted. And I say "us" very deliberately—I tried one of these before I bought Chauncy. Luckily for both of us, he had the sense to run away with me when I tried him out on cross-country so that I was under no illusions that he would be my schoolmaster!

4 You Are Two Peas in a Pod

"He and I are exactly alike."

Sometimes, having the same temperament as your horse is a good thing: that super-quiet draft horse is likely to love an equally laid-back rider. Two peas in a pod can be problematic, though, when you and your horse are equally high-strung.

I once met a rider who suffered from severe anxiety and panic attacks. Her horse was a lovely, sweet, well-bred Arabian who startled every time a bird flew by and couldn't stand still to save his life. Sadly, the two of them ricocheted off of each other's nervousness, one's Lizard Brain constantly triggered by the other's Lizard Brain, until they were both a mess, often before the poor woman even got on the horse. She was a fairly competent rider, and her horse always tried to do what he was asked, but their combined anxieties reached a critical mass so that neither of them could function optimally when they were together. Because Lizard Brains trigger each other so easily between humans and horses, humans who tend to be anxious are generally more successful with lower-octane horses.

5 The Vampire

In Stephanie Meyer's *Twilight* books and movie series, the handsome, brooding Edward turns out to be a vampire. He's a good vampire, though, with a deep soul and a big heart. He even sparkles. Bella falls for him and they discover that they are soul mates, eventually living happily ever after, except for some nasty business with a pack of werewolves.

The vampire horse sucks you in with the same qualities: he's devastatingly gorgeous, even sparkling, and his brooding nature makes you sure that there's a deep, misunderstood, but ultimately loving soul underneath his outer dangerous behavior. He may bite, kick, buck, or scrape you off on a wall, but you're sure you can get through to him if you only try hard enough. His beautiful movement and athleticism mesmerize you so much that you minimize the harm he's doing to your body and to your soul.

I know a gelding I'll call Jack. He is a drop-dead-gorgeous Hanoverian. He's 17.2 hands, a spectacular dark bay with one white sock and a perfect heart-shaped star. He floats over the ground as if he's gliding on air, and you can practically hear angels singing when he canters.

He's also a total vampire.

The minute a saddle goes on Jack's back, he morphs into evil incarnate. That lovely floating trot? It becomes a side-winding crab skittering along. If his rider puts her leg on, he kicks out and then bolts sideways. If she sits really quietly, he refuses to go forward—unless it's a Tuesday, in which case he half-rears and then bolts forward at top speed. At shows (yes, his rider has tried to show him), he is the menace of the warm-up ring, kicking out at other horses and jigging sideways. After 45 minutes or so, he usually settles down enough for his rider to get about 15 minutes of pleasant trot and canter. The next day, it starts all over again.

When I asked his rider why she keeps him, she replied, "He's just so beautiful, and he's such a great mover. I just know if I can figure him out, he'll be a great horse."

Here's the thing: Jack is not Edward. He's just a vampire. He's beautiful, but he's going to do what vampires do: suck you completely dry. Some riders can deal with a vampire's behavior if his performance in the show ring is exceptional. The great racehorse and Thoroughbred sire Nasrullah, for example, was notoriously cranky, exasperating, and even dangerous to his riders and trainers, but he was a brilliant runner when he chose to be, so they dealt with it. However, if you are like most of us and want your relationship with your horse to be a happy one, a vampire is always going to be a beautiful heartbreaker—or worse, he will hurt you someday.

6 The Abusive Boyfriend

You know you're in an abusive horse-and-rider relationship if you alternate between total elation and abject misery, and if you have no idea what brings out either the stellar or the despicable behavior in your horse. Between humans, abusive relationships are characterized by one person becoming nasty or violent for apparently minor reasons, or seemingly no reason at all. These incidents are interspersed with days of perfect behavior and relationship bliss, and they occur just often enough to keep the victim hoping that he or she can just do the right things at the right times in the right combinations to get the abuser to behave wonderfully all the time.

"Abusive boyfriend" horses are the same way: horrible one day, perfect the next. The problem is, sometimes something works, and then the next day, it doesn't. You can't find a pattern, because there probably isn't one. You end up feeling crazy.

Unlike in human-to-human relationships, horses don't intentionally manipulate people and make them feel crazy. Often, when a horse is acting like an abusive boyfriend, he's either in pain or in the wrong job. One such horse in our program went from an unpredictable heartbreaker as a show horse to a total Steady Eddie as a trail mount. He had been good enough often enough that we'd given him chance after chance, adjusting every single aspect of his program, trying to find the magic combination. His rider finally threw in the towel after he refused a jump he'd done dozens of times before, for no reason whatsoever. In his new life, he's as happy and confident as he can be.

If you suspect you and your horse are in an abusive cycle, give yourself permission to say enough is enough. Listen when people tell you that enough is enough. While I'm glad I got such great dressage experience with my Dutch mare after she resigned from eventing, I also spent a lot of months spinning my wheels and feeling heartbroken and worthless. Those months left a mark that stays with me still. If you can't bring yourself to "give up" on your horse, consider that you may actually be doing what's best for him by finding him a new job that suits him better.

7 But I Love Him!

"All You Need Is Love" is a classic Beatles tune, but it's woefully inadequate as a training philosophy. I hear this often from people who have, on impulse, "rescued" or otherwise taken on a horse from an apparently bad situation. While it can be a kind thing to do when you have the right experience and skill, it's often done without realizing that horses in negative situations often have negative behaviors to match, just as traumatized children often have severe behavior problems.

If you find that your heart is bigger than your training toolbox, please, *please* seek help from someone qualified to handle behavior problems. Don't just watch a few Natural Horsemanship videos or talk to someone who went to a Clinton Anderson clinic last year. Incomplete knowledge leads to inconsistent training, which leads to more (and possibly more severe and more dangerous) behavior problems.

It's easy to make things worse, despite the best possible intentions. Horses that have been abused, neglected, or traumatized in some way often need very specialized training that differs significantly from what we normally do with healthy horses. You may also find that a rescue horse needs more veterinary care than you expected. Ulcers, a sore back, or neglected teeth and hooves may need extensive treatment in order to address the horse's behavior.

"Love" is the reason given why people stick with most mismatched horses for too long. But think of it this way: if your best friend were in a terrible marriage, and she justified it by saying, "But I love my spouse," what would you tell her? Most likely, you'd tell her that love isn't enough to fix a bad relationship. And you'd be right. Love is important, but it's not enough.

8 The Horse for the Rider You Used to Be

In my twenties, I would—and could, and did—ride anything. Bucking, rearing, spinning were all challenges I took on with enthusiasm. I liked the badass reputation it gave me to sit on the horses that no one else wanted to ride.

Fast-forward twenty years. Add one marriage, two mortgages, a few dramatic falls, and a round of breast cancer, and there's *no way* I'd sit on many of those horses today—and I ride for a living! I still like my horses on the hot side, but if they are likely to put me on the ground on a regular basis, I pass them on to someone who's a version of the younger me.

This was not as easy as it sounds. My ego did not go down quietly. I still feel a twinge of failure when I pass up a request to work with a problem horse. However, I have different priorities now, and I recognize that I don't have to prove I'm a badass in order to feel good about myself as a rider.

I have spoken with many women in the same position. "This horse's shenanigans would have made me laugh when I was 14 years old. Why do they intimidate me now?" they demand. As I've mentioned earlier, our life experience changes who we are as riders. The older we are, the more awareness we have of our own mortality; we know people who have had serious injuries, and we may have had some of our own.

If you have children, you undoubtedly feel the weight of that responsibility as well. While our ego may sting a bit when we choose an "easier" ride, there is much more enjoyment in riding the horse that suits our current self. It's a little bit like giving up boy bands—I may sing along when Duran Duran plays on the radio, but I don't plaster my walls with posters of them anymore!

I'M RIDING THE WRONG HORSE—NOW WHAT?

You've found yourself in the descriptions above, or you have another variety of clash between you and your horse. What do you do now? Parting ways is not the only solution. Depending on the situation, there may be a way to work things out.

Get Professional Help

The simplest and most straightforward answer is to seek out more training for your horse, yourself, or both. If your horse is several steps ahead of or behind you in his experience, this is usually the best way forward. Ideally, you should take lessons not only on your own horse, but on a competent schoolmaster. It's much easier to focus on improving your own skills when you don't have to worry about whether the horse understands his job, or if you're undermining previous training on a well-trained but sensitive horse who can't forgive your mistakes.

In addition to your own lessons, get your trainer to ride your horse. Even if you can't afford to put him in full training, have him ridden at least a couple of times a month by an experienced professional. You can't teach someone to speak French if all you know is "Bonjour," and you can't train a horse to respond correctly if you are still learning your balance or don't know how to ask correctly for a canter depart.

Please understand, I am not saying you need to be a professional to train your own horse. The old saying is "Green plus green equals black and blue," but there are different kinds of green riders and green horses. My point is, recognize your limitations and the gaps in your knowledge, and know when to ask for help.

If the problem is more serious than just a training mismatch, expert help is absolutely essential. Dangerous or deeply entrenched misbehavior can be quite difficult to change, and just because someone is a good rider does not mean she has the skills to correct serious problems. For example, I usually can get a fearful horse that stops at jumps to start jumping confidently. Horses that rear, however, are above my pay grade. I don't have the skill set or the personality type to fix them, so I refer them to someone else. Likewise, the local teenage daredevil may be able to reform a rodeo-bronc-wannabe, but she probably doesn't have the mileage to retrain a horse that is terrified after a jumping accident.

Do plenty of research to make sure the trainer you hire is qualified to handle your situation. This may mean one trainer for you and another for your horse, or two trainers to work on different issues. My co-trainer Mary and I handle riding problems at our farm, but if a horse has issues with ground manners or trailer loading, our third partner

LIZZY AND KAREN'S STORIES:
TWO SHADES OF GREEN

Lizzy is my working student. She just turned 15, and she has been riding since she was six, mostly the difficult horses that no one else wants to ride. As a result, she can stay on absolutely anything. The girl seriously has a seat of glue.

When Lizzy was 12, she outgrew the pony she was leasing at our barn, and we needed to find her a new horse. Since she didn't have a big budget, we bought a green, off-the-track Thoroughbred for her, a horse a colleague of mine had been working with.

Normally, I would never put a 12-year-old on a greenie, let alone an ex-racehorse. However, Lizzy not only has a great seat, but she takes regular lessons and sees me every day. She is also much more patient than most kids her age (with horses, anyway). Because I can help her as much as she needs me to, and because of her background and personality, a green horse (from a source I trust) was a workable solution. Three years later, they are a terrific pair, showing and doing Pony Club together.

Karen, on the other hand, is a different shade of green. Whereas Lizzy was green at training a horse, Karen is still green in her balance and in her general riding ability. She works very hard and is making great progress, but she doesn't have "stickability" yet.

Karen also has a limited budget, and she has been eyeing the ads for the lovely horses that are retiring from the racetrack and have a low price tag. However, because she doesn't yet have any experience with quick-minded and quick-moving young horses, the ex-racehorse route is the wrong one for her right now. I am encouraging her instead to search for horses that are experienced but affordable because they are a bit older, a bit less flashy, or require some extra soundness maintenance. They may be less glamorous, but they will be much safer and much more enjoyable mounts for her at this stage of her riding career.

Chris takes over. No one is better at getting a rude, belligerent horse to lead quietly and stand still when he is asked, so we always defer to her in that realm.

Resist the Temptation to Skimp

A word about time, and a few words about money: good training takes time. Successful retraining usually takes more time. Becoming a good trainer takes years of dedication. Because of all of this, good training costs money. Period. You wouldn't expect to get a safe, reliable car for $200, and you shouldn't expect a competent trainer to come cheaply. If you are committed to keeping a horse that hasn't been working out for whatever reason, you need to be prepared for the fact that is likely to be expensive.

Cutting corners will land you in even more trouble in the long run. Do your homework before you start work with someone so that you know what to expect financially, and be honest with yourself and with the trainer about what your budget can handle. You may need to decide if you truly want to embark on a training endeavor, or if you are better off cutting your losses and moving on.

Handling High Octane—Yours and His

The "two-peas-in-a-pod" problem (p. 165) is one that does not lend itself easily to the training solutions I've just discussed. When you have a high-octane horse, chances are good that he is going to remain high-octane, and if you are an intense type yourself, you are not likely to undergo a major personality transformation, either. (Nor should you—there's nothing wrong with being high-octane!) There are some avenues for change worth trying, however, if you are committed to making this intense relationship work.

First, call your vet and do a full physical workup. Gastric ulcers, sore hocks, back pain, Lyme disease, and nutritional imbalances often contribute to behavioral issues. If you have a mare, she may need some management of her reproductive cycle to make her more comfortable and less edgy. Cushing's syndrome and other metabolic or hormonal disorders can impact behavior as well. Make sure you are doing everything possible for your horse's physical well-being to ensure that he can show you his true self.

When it comes to high-octane management, the personality you have the most control over is your own. Let's face it: your horse isn't lying in his stall at night, thinking, "Gosh, I'm way too tightly wound. I need to chill out and handle my stress more effectively. Maybe I'll try meditation." If you want things to improve, you are the one who will have to make some changes.

Horses can and will bring to light every single emotional and interpersonal issue we have. Every. Single. One. So, if high anxiety or a quick temper is a problem in your riding, I'm willing to bet it shows up in other parts of your life as well. There are two pieces of good news in this statement: 1) If you manage it effectively in other areas, you can use those same skills with your horse; and 2) any type of coping skills training can be shaped to work in your riding.

Do What Already Works

How do you handle your intensity in the rest of your life? Notice what you do, and try these things before and during your rides.

• If you pause and take a breath before replying to an irritating comment, do the same when your horse spooks at a butterfly.

• If you blast hip-hop music or Mozart on your evening commute to help you de-stress, do the same on the way to the barn.

• If you usually vent about your day when you get home so you can have a relaxing evening, vent to your horse while you're brushing him, so your stress doesn't carry over into your ride.

Exercise is a great way to decrease anxiety, so do a little cardio before coming to the barn, or start your ride with an energetic canter that gets your heart pumping.

Get Outside Help

If intense emotion is a pervasive problem in your life, there are plenty of excellent resources to help you manage your feelings more effectively. Mindfulness Based Stress Reduction (MBSR) is proven to reduce stress and anxiety significantly, and is taught in communities around the country. Cognitive-behavioral therapy and mindfulness meditation are also very effective for decreasing anxiety and improving emotional resilience. There are many self-help books on the subject as well. As you learn to manage and soothe your Lizard Brain more successfully, you will become less reactive to your horse's intensity, and more able to soothe him when he becomes anxious.

Switch It Up

If your horse makes it clear that he hates the job you've chosen for him and nothing is going to change that, you can choose to switch disciplines. This is an excellent option if, like the student I mentioned earlier, you love this horse more than you love your chosen type of riding. One wonderful aspect of the equestrian world is the myriad options we have: driving, reining, trail riding, vaulting, dressage, jumping, cowboy mounted shooting—the list goes on. Use this situation as an opportunity to try something new. I have even seen a few Vampires transform into happy horses when given a new job.

Along those same lines, you don't have to do *anything* with your horse if you so choose. If you adore him, but he's too old, too injured, too hot, too cranky, too whatever to be anything but a pasture pet, then he can be a pasture pet. If you are happy to have him in your life in that capacity, then by all means, do so. Don't expect other people to understand, but they don't have to. It's *your* horse, so as long as you can interact with him safely, you get to decide how he fits into your life.

Step Away from the Keyboard

If you are into social media, you may be tempted to ask people online about what you should do about your horse. Please, in the name of all that is holy, DON'T DO IT. Just don't. Read the threads of others with similar problems if you must, but just don't go swimming in those shark-infested waters. Inevitably, there will be several know-it-alls whose strong opinions are in direct inverse relationship to their knowledge and experience, and they will take it as their sacred duty to both advise and judge you.

Unlike asking people's opinions on the latest fly spray, talking about your dilemma online leaves you emotionally exposed and vulnerable to people who have not earned the privilege of seeing that vulnerability. You'll also just get a lot of really bad advice. Gathering multiple points of view is often helpful, but make sure they come from people you respect, in private conversations that protect your privacy and vulnerability.

WHEN IT'S TIME TO MOVE ON

Sometimes, all the training and patience and love and creativity in the world aren't enough, and it's time to let go of your horse. While I can't tell you when it's time, it's very likely that you will know when that day arrives. There is usually a small, quiet knowing that stands firm underneath the chaos of confusion, stress, and frustration. When you acknowledge it for the first time, there is usually an intense rush of grief, followed by a sense of relief. You will probably toggle back and forth between these two emotions at various times, but as you come to terms with them, you are likely to recognize that you are doing the best thing not only for yourself, but for your horse. When you are the wrong match for each other, the best thing you can do is to find the right one for each of you.

Selling and re-homing horses is not my area of expertise, so I won't attempt to give you any advice on this front. However, there are many resources available in local horse communities and online that can assist you with this process. As always, start with people you trust, and do thorough research.

Finding Mr. (or Ms.) Right: Don't Go It Alone

When you feel ready to search for your next equine partner, go back to the beginning of this chapter and write your Equine Personal Ad (p. 157). You can use this as your starting point to find a match that will, as one instructor said to me, "make you smile every day."

Horse shopping is exhilarating, stressful, and often brain-scrambling. You can do it alone, but why would you? It's far too easy to fall head over heels for some big, flashy-moving, beautiful bay with four white socks and a blaze, and have those George Clooney looks blind you to the fact that his hocks are a disaster or that he's three years greener than you are ready for.

Ideally, bring along a trainer you trust, preferably one who knows your riding and your personality. You should expect to pay for this service, but it is money well spent, and it can often prevent you from making a very expensive mistake. Many trainers have years of experience assessing horses, and they are likely to catch small details you might overlook. I always tell my students that they don't have to buy a horse if I like him but they don't, but I insist that they walk away if I see that the horse is unsuitable for them, because I'm seeing something problematic that isn't obvious to them. Trust and communication are critical here, of course; before we even look at any horses, we discuss thoroughly what their "personal ad" looks like, and we agree on what we want to avoid.

If you don't have a trainer to work with, bring along a knowledgeable and honest friend. Ideally, such a friend should be your temperamental opposite: if you're impulsive, she can put on the brakes; if you're indecisive, she can list objectively a horse's pros and cons. She needs to be confident enough to voice her disagreement with you, and not just tell you what you want to hear.

Make sure she respects your checkbook—this is *not* the time to call the person who talked you into two pairs of high heels and some earrings when you went out to buy a sweater! Most of all, the person needs to be a good sounding board who can help you sort through your thoughts and a large amount of information.

I'll leave you with a bit of wisdom I overheard at someone's lesson many years ago. The rider was trying to get the horse to cooperate, and the horse was having none of it, thank you very much. Finally, the trainer stopped, put his hand on the rider's knee, and said, "Sweetheart, there are so many wonderful horses in the world that love to do this job. Why are you insisting on forcing this one to do a job he obviously hates? You both deserve better than this."

Happy horse hunting.

PART IV

StressLess Techniques
for Trainers

Make the Brain
Your Ally

WANTED: Riding instructor for busy riding stable. Excellent riding skills and show record required. Must be good with children, prickly adolescents, and overstressed adults of all riding levels. Ability to de-escalate emotional outbursts a plus. Must be available seven days a week, both in person and over the phone, during lessons and after hours. Additional duties include filling in for unreliable barn help, managing over-competitive parents, motivating indifferent kids, and sourcing horses and ponies that will never bite, buck, or bolt. One half-day off, once per month, except during show season, which runs from March through November. Salary might cover your rent, or it might not. Cheerful attitude a must.

Does this job description sound familiar? And that's just a normal Tuesday for many of us. Most of us in the equestrian world are riders first and teachers second; otherwise, we would be in a classroom instead of the barn. We have the incredibly challenging and delicate task of educating both horses and riders, and few trainers have had formal education in instructional theory or human behavior to use as a guide.

From my vantage point as both a therapist and a riding instructor, one reality is clear to me: every emotional, relational, and social issue in a rider's life eventually shows up in the riding arena. Every. Single.

One. Horses challenge us in all of these realms, often to a far greater extent than other sports will ever do. A golfer might look foolish if she gets frustrated and throws a club, but the golf club isn't going to bite or kick her in retaliation. When a skier breaks a ski pole, she can throw it away and buy a new one. A rider, on the other hand, has to learn to cope effectively with her frustration, or it negatively impacts the horse as well as her performance. If her horse is injured or ruined through poor riding or abusive treatment, that horse can't just be tossed away and replaced.

By virtue of having a living creature as "sports equipment," riders have to learn to overcome personal limitations, emotional challenges, and communication difficulties in order to be successful. This means that to be effective trainers, we need to understand not just the mind of the horse, but the mind of the rider as well. This chapter will help you get a handle on some of the common issues and problems we face with our students.

TIMES REALLY HAVE CHANGED

The equestrian circles on social media are rife with various rants on the theme, "Back in the Good Old Days." You know the ones I mean:

"Kids today have no work ethic."

"In my day, we were happy to scrub buckets till 7:00 p.m. and then ride in the dark."

"We trained our own horses back then. We didn't have made horses handed to us."

And so on and so forth, ad infinitum. "Back then" is viewed as The Golden Age of Horsemanship, and current riders are seen as sloppy, lazy, and spoiled. True? In some cases, probably. But to quote an old Billy Joel song, "The good old days weren't always good, tomorrow ain't as bad as it seems." Many modern training and teaching methods are an improvement over old ones, and it is possible to have hard-working, motivated students. Understanding the way the world has changed can help you craft an effective teaching methodology for the modern rider.

Many trainers lament the "laziness" they see in current students. They complain that riders want instant results, they have poor frustration tolerance, and they give up easily. I would argue, however, that this is not about sloth as a character flaw. Instead, it's a result of rapid cultural shifts, particularly around technology.

As I write this, my iPhone is next to me, my Facebook page is open on my computer, and my iPad is open so I can reference a book I've just downloaded. And I'm by no means a tech geek! In the space of a couple of decades, our entire world has shifted so that it revolves around technology. I have access to any information I want by touching a screen a few times—I don't even have to go across the room to the bookshelf, let alone actually leave the house and go to a library to do my research. It's not your imagination; the world really *is* moving faster and faster, it's easier to get what you want when you want it, and there are more and more bits of information being hurled at us all day long.

All of this easy access and rapid-fire stimulation has an impact on the structure and functioning of our brains. The science is in its early stages, but so far, it's indicating some very important trends: 1) The more instant gratification we get, the less "struggle muscle" we tend to exert; and 2) the more rapid-fire stimulation our brains get, the more we want. No wonder people new to the sport expect instant results—they get them everywhere else in their life!

Riding often runs directly counter to this process: it's very hard work at times, and it takes a lot of time to get good at it. This can be frustrating and discouraging to people who don't have to flex their struggle muscles very often in everyday life. As trainers growing up in the pre-screen age, most of us learned quite early that we had to put in tremendous effort for long periods of time, so we sometimes have trouble relating to this. It's the same feeling, though, that I get when my computer screen freezes up—I don't want to have to learn about computers, I just want the damn thing to do what I want it to do!

The other major shift that affects trainers is the change in demographics. Most riders don't grow up around horses anymore; it's an extra-curricular activity, not an integral part of the fabric of their world. Many of our students are the first ones in their family to learn to ride. Also, many more people are taking up or returning to riding in adulthood. Riding for them is an escape from stress, a refuge from the demands and pressures of the outside world. When it doesn't go well, it feels like one more stressor instead of an escape, and they feel frustrated and disappointed.

Does this mean we should just give in, go find our students "perfect" horses, and make sure we keep them entertained? No way. But it does mean we need to understand that we are asking people to do the complete opposite of what they do all day long, and so it's going to be mentally and physically hard for them. Even sitting up straight can be hard—where else in modern life do we need such perfect posture? If we remember that it's hard for them, we are less likely to see our riders as "lazy," and more likely to show them that there is a deep sense of fulfillment that comes from doing hard things.

MAKING HARD "FUN"

Imagine you are interested in taking up a new activity. You go online to find out more about it, and you read descriptions like this:

"There is a lot of slogging along in the trenches, which is why so few have the stomach for the process of getting good…"

"Endless hours learning to lose, being disappointed multiples times…"

"Trudging outside in the cold before dawn each morning to shovel manure…"

"Too many kids haven't been taught about the work it takes…"

Are you thinking what I'm thinking? SIGN ME UP FOR THAT! Yeah, right, in Purgatory maybe. Right after I stack 7,000 cords of firewood and have beets for dinner.

Look, we all know riding is hard work, but that's not *why* we do it! Stacking wood is hard, and it sucks. We don't do it to work hard; we do it to stay warm. In riding, we work hard for the fulfillment and exhilaration that come from doing the work to ride well. Without that, there's no point to the hard work. We need to do a better job of communicating that exhilaration to our students so that they have a *reason* to work hard.

"I shouldn't have to make it 'fun' all the time," trainers have complained to me. Well, why not? Our students are riding—and paying us to teach them—*for enjoyment.* What we need to show them is that "hard" and "fun" are not mutually exclusive. Share your own experiences with them. Tell your students about your own efforts and how amazing it feels when you accomplish a goal. Let them see your own excitement when you solve a tough training problem or fix a stubborn position flaw. Encourage them to get excited about successful moments: "There, can you feel his back swing now? Doesn't that feel cool?" Point out how their persistence has paid off: "You just killed it over that course! Remember when you thought those jumps looked huge and terrifying?"

Motivation comes from connecting our efforts with positive outcomes. Help your students see the connection between their efforts and their enjoyment, and you will see their motivation expand.

KNOW THYSELF

Who are you as a trainer? Do you love to teach kids, or are adults more your style? Do you excel at bringing beginners into the sport, or do you prefer to teach competitive riders? Are you very hands-on about your students' choice of horses and their riding goals, or do you follow their lead and focus on their priorities? Understanding yourself as a trainer is a vital part of building a satisfying career; when you know yourself, you'll know who your ideal students are, and you can focus on attracting those riders to your program.

Exercise: Your Training Personality

Answer the following questions on paper or a tablet in as much detail as possible. When you finish, you will have a better picture of who you are and what motivates you as a trainer.

1 Think of three of your favorite students, past or present. What do they have in common, and how are they different? What do you enjoy most about teaching them?

2 What was your favorite teaching moment in the last few weeks? What made it stand out?

3 Think of a student you have a hard time teaching. What makes it difficult? How do you feel when you are teaching him or her?

4 When you are teaching, do you focus more on what the rider is doing, or how the horse is going?

5 If you had to quit teaching today, what would you miss most?

Notice any repeating themes in your answers? I love working with students who are very interactive and speak up in lessons, while I struggle with reserved, quiet people, especially if I can't read their body language. I get excited when riders want to know why they're doing what I've told them to do.

Pay attention to how you feel as you answer these questions. Our horses trust their feelings to guide them 100 percent of the time. When we are similarly aware of how we feel, our instincts and intuition can surface, helping us choose the best path for ourselves as trainers. Our work, our students, and our horses can only benefit from that deeper knowledge.

Now let's talk teaching methods. Regardless of the type of instructor you are and who your ideal students are, some teaching methods are more effective than others. I'm not talking about whether you use draw reins or standing martingales or what types of bits are most effective for a strong horse; there are tons of other books on those subjects. I'm talking about the way that you convey all of that knowledge to your students: the language you use, the way you communicate, how your students hear what you have to say.

POSITIVE TEACHING: WHAT IT IS, WHY IT MATTERS

"Good job!" is probably the phrase most people imagine when they think of "positive teaching." Positive teachers do offer praise and encouragement, and their students usually feel good when they finish a lesson. However, it's much more than simply making people feel good about themselves. Positive teaching allows the trainer to create better riders, because it taps into the strengths of the human brain efficiently and effectively.

Go to any online discussion forum or eavesdrop on any tack-room conversation, and inevitably you'll hear complaints about trainers who are too negative. "Big Name Trainer 'A' told Rider 'X' she was too fat." "Big Name Rider 'B' told Rider 'Y' that she'd rather ride a rhinoceros than ride his horse." Negativity and nastiness definitely earn some trainers a bad name, and legitimately so.

On the other hand, "Susie Sunshine" trainers get criticized for allowing riders to coast along in their comfort zones, never challenging, always praising, whether the praise is warranted or not. This tends to be the stereotypical image of "positive" teaching. It grew out of the cringe-worthy self-esteem movement of the 1990s, the one that praised 15-year-olds for brushing their teeth and never criticized them for fear of damaging that oh-so-fragile self-esteem.

Where is the right balance? There are coaches in our sport and in many others who are described as tyrannical, insulting, not afraid to break your eggs to make their omelet. They scream, they rant, they throw things when displeased. Yet, some are considered the greatest coaches of all time. They aren't winning any charm awards, but they manage to draw the best out of their athletes. They are frequently cited in complaints of "kids today are too soft."

Do they get results? Yes, from a select few elite athletes, usually ones who are extremely thick-skinned by nature and are hell-bent on making it to the Olympics. But I believe this is mostly in spite of, rather than because of, their raging and blustering, and they probably lose some extremely talented athletes due to this behavior. And for most of us as instructors and trainers, this behavior is *much* less effective than Positive Teaching methods.

Positive Teaching is *not* telling people they are doing a great job, whether they are or not, or praising their efforts, regardless of whether those efforts produce results. It's not telling people, "That's okay," when their performance was really terrible or they didn't bother to expend any effort. It's not giving everyone a ribbon every time. In fact, praise and reward have been proven detrimental to performance if they are disconnected from significant effort: if you get a ribbon for everything, ribbons lose their meaning, so why bother to try for one?

In the movie *The Incredibles*, mom Helen (a retired superhero) tells her son Dash (a budding superhero) that "everyone's special." He sneers, "That's just another way of saying nobody is." We also know that people need difficult challenges to improve. And in riding, if you're never pushed at all, you never develop the mental toughness to handle a half-ton flight animal whose opinions often differ from yours.

So if Positive Teaching isn't all sunshine and flowers, what is it? In my view, a Positive Teacher does four things:

1 She tells riders what to do and how to do it.

2 She criticizes the riding without attacking the rider.

3 She encourages students and expresses confidence in their ability to succeed.

4 She challenges riders without over-facing them.

Let's expand on each of these four factors and how they play out in a typical lesson or coaching situation.

1 Tell the Student What to Do and How to Do It

This may seem obvious—it's the definition of teaching—but many trainers make mistakes here. When I walk courses at horse trials, I often hear phrases such as, "Don't let him fall in here," or "Don't look down." This unfortunately creates the very behavior we want our students to avoid.

Remember the purple elephant exercise on page 81? The brain can't visualize a "not" or a negative. It has to picture the thing (looking down), then figure out what to picture instead of the thing (where should I look?). It's more effective to say, "Keep him to the outside on this turn," or "Look up." When you point out what the student is doing wrong, for example, "Don't lean forward," follow it with what you want her to do instead: "Sit tall."

Similarly, when giving instructions, tell the rider *how* to do what you're asking. Remember, you know more than she does—what is obvious or automatic to you is not necessarily so to your student. You may need to get on the horse and do what you want the rider to do in order to figure out exactly what you're doing to make it happen. Thus, "Make him straight," might need to be, "He's swinging his haunches to the left, so put your left leg on just behind the girth to make him straight."

You may need to try multiple ways of phrasing something until you find what works with a particular person. Develop a big vocabulary and a wide range of metaphors, and use humor whenever possible—for some reason, humor makes a concept really stick.

2 Criticize the Riding, Not the Rider

Someone I know was told by a trainer, "I don't know why you bother trying to learn to ride." She also told people they were hopeless and pathetic. Needless to say, these comments didn't improve the rider's seat, nor did it help the trainer's business, as none of those people ride with her any longer.

On the flip side, I overheard a trainer at a show say something like this after a poor dressage test: "We planned that you would ride conservatively in your trot lengthening. You got overexcited and pushed too much, and he broke to canter. Next time, you need to take it easy, so the movement is correct even if it's not flamboyant." This trainer held his rider accountable for her mistakes, but he criticized her actions, rather than launching a personal attack. The rider was clearly chagrined, but knew exactly what she needed to do in order to improve the next ride.

This step isn't about being a nice person (though that always helps); it's about avoiding the trip wire that activates the Lizard Brain's Fight or Flight Response. When we feel personally attacked, embarrassed, or shamed, the Fight or Flight Response is triggered instantaneously, and the Lizard Brain grabs the reins and hijacks the ride. Once this occurs, the rider's ability to think clearly and to process language is significantly compromised, as her Rational Brain gets bypassed. She becomes defensive and argumentative (fight), or she cries and shuts down (flight). At that point, the trainer has lost the student and the teaching moment.

On the other hand, if a trainer points out what was wrong with the riding and helps the rider find a way to solve the problem, the rider can feel empowered instead of attacked. This allows her to move forward and improve instead of feeling shamed and shutting down.

A few words about using shame as a way to force someone to change: Don't. Just don't. Shame is anything that makes someone feel small, or that they are innately bad, stupid, or worthless. It is one of the most powerful emotions in the spectrum of human feeling, and it makes people either crawl under a rock or charge forward in full-frontal attack mode. Spend a few seconds recalling a time when you felt shamed, and you'll know exactly what I'm talking about. Research shows that shame virtually never motivates positive behavior, so don't go there. And if you do go there (we all lose our cool sometimes), apologize as soon as possible. Shame is the most toxic emotion out there, and it leaves behind damage that is very difficult to repair.

Political Correctness vs. Building Trust

At this point, you may feel like we've slipped into Political Correctness Hell. Do we really have to tiptoe around, worrying about hurting someone's feelings every second? No—not as long as we've laid a good foundation of trust with our students. Let me give you some examples.

Exhibit A: Famous Clinician Who Shall Not Be Named spends five minutes evaluating a student (Rider A) in a clinic and snarls, "Maybe God will perform a miracle and you'll suddenly be able to ride."

Exhibit B: Another Famous Clinician works with Rider B every couple of months for two years; the rider has made steady progress, and AFC both validates progress and pushes the rider to do more. Rider has a terrible round and says to AFC, "I get nervous when the jumps get that big." AFC retorts, "Well, then, you'll need to toughen the f--- up and get your s—together, won't you?"

Two seemingly nasty comments, but the first sends a rider into a tailspin, while the second makes the rider redouble her efforts and produce a great second round. What's the difference?

Trust.

Rider B has developed a relationship with AFC over time, and knows that AFC is invested in her success. When AFC tells Rider B in colorful terms that she needs to get her act together, Rider B trusts not only that AFC is right, but that AFC believes she can do it. AFC also knows Rider B well enough to know that she can handle tough language and that it will push her to succeed.

Meanwhile, Rider A is feeling demoralized because she has been attacked personally before she's even had a chance for her butterflies to settle. Famous Clinician's words cause her to freeze up, because there is no relationship between them, and she can't trust that FC is in her corner and wants her to succeed.

When riders trust you, you can be incredibly tough on them and they will rise to the occasion. They trust that you are being tough because you know they will use it to motivate themselves, rather than because you think they're pathetic and you're trying to humiliate them. Relationship and trust are the foundation of everything else.

3 Encourage Students and Express Your Confidence in Their Ability to Succeed

The flip side of criticism is encouragement. We all need both to become competent riders. Encouragement is different from praise. Praise is telling someone that they did a good job; encouragement is exhorting someone to persevere, to keep trying when something is difficult. It lets our students know that we believe in them, that we are confident that they can accomplish what they are attempting, even if it's taking a long time to get there and they're making a lot of mistakes. Encouragement promotes mental toughness and the development of struggle muscle, which helps people keep going in the face of difficulty.

Research confirms the importance of encouragement. Studies of resilient adults aim to identify what makes some people able to thrive despite severe adversity—abuse, homelessness, early loss of parents, and so on. In repeated studies, the vast majority of resilient adults named at least one person in their lives who encouraged them and expressed faith in their ability to succeed. Encouragement is one of our most powerful tools as teachers.

You don't have to turn into a loud, perky cheerleader to encourage your students. Do it in a way that suits your personality and the needs of your particular student. The rider who was told to "toughen the f--- up" felt encouraged at that moment, because she and the clinician had developed a tough-talking relationship, and it worked for both of them. Other riders obviously need a different approach. The important thing is to communicate to your riders, "I know you can do this. Stick with it."

4 Challenge, Don't Overface

This is a bit of an art form. Students need to be pushed past their comfort zone, but not pushed far enough to scare them into a setback. How do you walk this line successfully?

With new students, or with riders in a clinic who you are unlikely to see frequently, less is more. You are better off under-challenging someone new than risking that you'll push her too far. When in doubt, ask: "How are you doing? Does this feel too hard, or too easy?" I tell new students that they can always ask me to take things down a notch. We can always turn up the heat later, but if you over-face someone, you now have a new problem to fix.

With regular students, you will have a better sense of how far to push. The main thing to remember is that challenge doesn't always feel good or comfortable. Point this out to your students as well: "It's fine that this feels awkward right now. I'm raising the bar on you. It will get easier, don't worry." Watch body language: if you see increased muscle and facial tension or a blank expression, it may be a warning sign to slow down.

Your relationship with your students matters a great deal here. You can push harder when you have built that foundation of trust; this takes longer with some people than with others. Some people are also hard-wired to be more anxious and more cautious than others. Notice whether a student tends to jump right into new things, or if she needs time to get used to an idea, and adjust the level of challenge accordingly. Make a point of emphasizing progress: "You were so sure you couldn't do that, but you just did!" It's similar to recognizing how much to push a particular horse based on his temperament: you take more time with the sensitive one and let him get used to things before you ask for more demanding work.

I sum up my philosophy of challenge by telling my students, "I won't ask you to do anything you aren't capable of doing. I *will* ask you to do lots of things you *think* you aren't capable of doing." This helps me stay just outside my students' comfort zone, which is where the greatest learning can occur.

THE NOT-SO-MAGNIFICENT SEVEN

Before I wrote this chapter, I took a highly unscientific poll of my training colleagues and asked them what their biggest challenges were with their students. There was a wide variety of responses, but some common themes definitely stood out. Here are the ones that people mentioned the most, with some ideas about how to handle them effectively.

1 Deer in the Headlights
This phenomenon happens most often in competition situations but can occur anytime a student is highly stressed. Some students are hijacked

so completely by their Lizard Brain when under stress that their eyes go blank, they wear a dazed expression, and they don't appear to hear a thing you are saying. They may ride erratically, with little or no control; they seem to have checked out completely.

In this case, things are actually exactly as they seem: the student *has* checked out. Review the Fight of Flight Response in chapter 1 (p. 16) for a full explanation, but in a nutshell, the student's Rational Brain has been shut down and the Lizard Brain is now running the show. You have to help the rider slow down her Fight or Flight Response enough that she can think clearly again, so she can do what she knows how to do.

First, get the rider's attention: say her name, and ask if she can hear you. Make sure she answers verbally and doesn't just nod. If possible, get her to stop her horse and stand still. Make eye contact, and tell her to breathe. Next, tell her what you see happening. "Jess, you seem to have checked out and your Lizard Brain is trying to take over. Why don't you take a few more deep breaths—I don't think you've done that for a little while. Then we'll figure out what to do next." If she has trouble making eye contact, put your hand on her boot or on her wrist—touch helps people ground themselves when their Fight or Flight Response is in charge. She may need to walk around for a few minutes before she can move on.

Once you have her attention, you can get her to problem-solve and plan. Ask what is happening between her and her horse, without letting her go into lengthy explanations or over-analysis of the situation. Once she has done this, ask what she can do to improve the situation. Make sure it's specific, such as "slow the tempo," rather than something vague, such as "I need to relax." Before she starts to ride again, give her a specific instruction—"Circle around me in the slowest trot you can produce"—and get her to repeat the instruction back to you, so you know that her Rational Brain is back on track. As you coach her through the next few minutes, use her name frequently, remind her to breathe, and have her respond verbally to you to keep her firmly in her Rational Brain.

2 Blind Ambition

This student wants to move up the levels too fast. She wants to jump 3'6", but you put her competence around 3 feet. Often, this rider has recently purchased a horse that has competed at a more advanced level than the rider has. Or, she has ridden in a clinic with the Big Name Rider of the Season who had her doing more advanced movements or bigger jumps. She has won some ribbons and her qualifying scores to move up, but you know there are gaps in her skills that will come back to bite her at the next level. What should you do?

The first priority is safety. If you know that a student won't be safe at the next level, it's a no-go. Period. Usually, if you are dealing with a child or teenager, explaining your concerns to the parents will do the trick, but not always. Be ready to have specific examples of your concerns if you want to make your point. The student's argument is usually that if she is schooling this level at home, she should be able to handle it in competition. As we know, that is not always true. I try to come up with exercises that simulate the real challenge of competition. For example, if she is schooling 3'3" but I don't think she is ready to jump this height in competition, I'll set up an entire course at that height. If she can ride it smoothly and in control, three times in a row, then I will consider letting her compete at the higher level. If not, I explain clearly what isn't working and why it's a problem. I also tell her what she needs to do to show me that she is ready to move up in the future so that she has a clear road map for moving forward. Explanations can also circumvent power struggles, because you can make it clear that you want your student to be safe and successful.

What if the student signs up for the next level anyway? Your response depends partly upon your coaching style. When it comes to safety, I am non-negotiable. Before they even start competing, I tell my students that I have veto power over any show if I feel they will be unsafe or the horse will be at risk. If they insist anyway, I won't coach them at the show.

Some trainers aren't comfortable being this strict; if you are in this category, you need to consider several things. One, what is your responsibility if the student gets hurt? Two, are you risking your reputation as an instructor by sending an under-qualified student into the ring? And three, is your fear of losing a student overriding your judgment that this is an unsafe situation? Remember that our students represent us, for better or worse, and accidents or scary riding will be remembered for a long time.

If safety isn't the primary concern, your job is much simpler. (Notice I didn't say easier!) If the rider is safe, but not quite up to snuff for the next level, the main risk is loss of face. In this situation, experience is usually the best teacher. Your job is to debrief afterward: How did that go? What went well, and what needs work? Video can be especially helpful here to illustrate your point. Is the rider missing the fundamental basics to ride at this level, or is she just green and needs more experience? Avoid anything that resembles "I told you so," and be willing to be surprised—sometimes we are being too conservative, and our students show us that they are better than we gave them credit for!

3 The Blame Game

In my highly unscientific poll, the most common complaint was about students who blame their horse when things aren't going well.

"He's not listening."

"He's being a jerk."

"I never have this problem on that other horse."

Sometimes the blame is just an expression of frustration on a particular day, but some riders make a habit of it. Some genuinely believe they haven't found the right horse, and many who have financial means will keep "upgrading" to a new one when they hit a wall. We can complain all we want about riders who don't take responsibility for their role in the problem, but in the end, it becomes our job as trainers to teach that responsibility to our students.

I blame Walt Disney, really. All of those talking animals—adorable Thumper and Bambi, evil-scheming Iago the parrot in *Aladdin*, goofy Dori the fish in *Finding Nemo*—they make us see our animals as people, no matter how much we know better. Think you're immune? Notice how you've talked to your dog today. We used to call one group of geldings the "Frat Boys." I often talk to my students about what a horse is thinking, and I use very human language to do it: "He's wondering whether he needs to take you seriously or not." We put value judgments on their behavior as well: we refer to them as team players, honest souls, hams. If we do this after years of experience, it shouldn't be surprising when a student takes the next step and ascribes negative motives to her horse's behavior.

It's important to teach our students that although we talk about horses' "thoughts," what they are driven by are feelings—happy, scared, content, confused. We need to explain that horses don't have evil motives because they aren't future-oriented; their consciousness exists only in the present. They have memories, but not long-term goals. On the flip side, they also aren't working for us out of the goodness of their heart, either. They work because we tell them to, not because they want to go to the Olympics someday.

I try to redirect blaming with something along the following lines: "I know it's frustrating when your horse doesn't seem to want to cooperate. But whether the problem is his fault or yours doesn't matter, because the solution is always the same: ride better. Your horse doesn't care about your goals. He cares about his food, his herd, and his turnout time. He's not lying in his stall at night, scheming about how to make your life miserable. On the other hand, he's not lying there thinking, 'Man, I was a real jerk in the ring today. I really ought to be more cooperative next time.' Horses don't care about performing; we do, so it's up to us to fix the problem."

In the moment, when the student is frustrated, don't get into a long lecture about how it's wrong to blame the horse. The student's Fight or Flight Response is already activated, and it's in Fight mode. When a lecture triggers guilt or shame, the rider is going to escalate more and think even less effectively. If the rider can't get unstuck, give her something easier to do, or end the lesson early. If blaming is a pattern, you can have a talk with the student at a calmer time, such as at the beginning of a lesson.

No matter how much you want to scold, unless the rider is really out of line, empathy is much more effective. You can be stern to get her attention: "Whoa, wait a second. Hold everything. This is getting out of hand." But if you want the rider to calm down enough to hear you, she needs to know you understand. "I get how frustrating it can be—I hate it when I feel like I'm doing all I can and it's not working." This lets the Lizard Brain back down from Fight mode, and then you can engage the Rational Brain in some problem-solving.

4 Excuses, Excuses

"It's too hot."

"It's too cold."

"The footing's bad."

"She's so stiff today."

"I did that, but it didn't work."

"I had a fight with my boyfriend today and I can't concentrate."

Is your head exploding yet? Excuses were Number 2 in my informal survey of instructor pet peeves.

For me, excuses are different from reasons. A reason is an explanation, but we take responsibility for what comes next: "I had a fight with my boyfriend today, and I'm still a train wreck. Let me try that sliding stop again." Excuses attempt to let us off the hook: "It's too hot. I can't possibly work in this weather." When our students offer excuses, our job is to act as if they're giving us a reason, and then return to them the responsibility for the solution. My three preferred methods for doing this are humor, the blasé reality check, and empathy.

Humor works best when you already have a good rapport with a student; otherwise, it comes off as sarcasm, which tends to shut people down. I've been guilty of crossing that line more than once, and it always backfires. If you can make a student laugh or at least smile, though, you can usually get back on track. My favorite line is some version of, "I know, right? Don't you wish the universe would get its act together and do things *our* way?"

The blasé reality check usually sounds something like this: "You're right, it is hard. Really hard. That's just riding—nothing will change that. If you want easy, you'll need to find another activity. But you've done hard things before, and you can do this, too." This does several things. It depersonalizes the difficulty—it's not something you are doing to the student, it's just the way the world works: water is wet, it gets dark at night, riding is hard sometimes. It also puts the responsibility for effort back on the rider, while expressing confidence that she can handle it. Lastly, when delivered in a calm, somewhat bland way, it ensures that you are not investing more emotional energy in the rider's choices than she is. If you want a student to take responsibility, you can't be the hardest-working person in the room.

Whose Goals Are They?

A word about emotional investment: make sure that what you're pushing for is part of the rider's goals, not what *you* want for her. Some riders simply aren't driven to excel or to compete; they just want to be competent enough to enjoy their horse. *There is nothing wrong with this.* If you always feel like the hardest-working person in the room, ask yourself whose goals you are pursuing. If they aren't the student's goals, you may need to take your expectations down a notch.

Empathy is woven into all of these responses to excuses, but sometimes, it's the only thing necessary to get back on track. If a normally hard-working rider is offering excuses, there may be something going on underneath the surface. Ask. It doesn't have to be a big deal. "Are you okay? You don't seem like yourself," is enough. If she is upset, you can let her vent, and offer a little empathy. "Ugh, I'm sorry, that sounds rough." Often, this helps the rider turn things around.

5 Over-Competitive Parents

A student's parent approaches you. He expresses frustration that his daughter doesn't try hard enough, isn't dedicated enough, doesn't win enough at shows. You know that the student likes to ride, but couldn't care less if she has ribbons on her stall door. Or maybe you even know that she wouldn't ride at all if given the choice. How do you handle parents whose goals are out of sync with what the child cares about?

Goal-setting is one way to clarify what a parent and child each expect from riding. This can be a formal sit-down talk where goals are written down, or it can be a casual chat at the beginning of a lesson (usually easier for the child). Ask the student some fundamental questions: Why are you riding? What do you like about it? What do you dislike? Where do you want to be at the end of the summer/in six months/in a year? Really push for specifics: if she tells you she rides because it's fun, find out what's fun about it. Does she love barrel racing, or does she love being with her friends? Does she love to show, or is she happy to spend hours brushing her pony?

Have a similar conversation with the parent: why do you want your child to ride? What do you want her to learn from it? Do you think your child wants the same things from riding that you want for her?

If you know a parent and child are at odds, you may want to have separate conversations with each of them and then talk about it together. If possible, highlight the similarities between their goals. Parent may want child to win and child may only want to be with her friends at the shows, but they both want child to have a good ride while she's there. If the child doesn't want to show at all but the parent wants her to do so, you might suggest a lighter show schedule or "taking a break" from showing until the child shows greater interest. You can point out to the parent that kids' interest in riding and competing tends to vacillate over time, and a child will perform better when her heart is in it. In the meantime, you can point out the other benefits of riding: exercise, positive body image, discipline, care for something other than herself.

In competition, one way to keep ribbon-focused parents in check is to articulate Process Goals (p. 110) and discuss them with both riders and their parents. Ribbons are Outcome Goals (p. 110) and are only marginally in our control. Process goals are specific skills and behaviors that riders need to get results: seeing a distance to a jump, sitting the trot, handling a horse's misbehavior calmly. When parents get overly focused on a child's placing, I remind them of the Process Goal: "Yes, that score needs to be higher in order for her to get a ribbon. She got closer to that today when she nailed all of her transitions."

Parents are under a lot of daily pressure to ensure that their children are "successful" in the world, and they are constantly comparing themselves to other parents by evaluating how their child is doing in comparison to others. Riding can become another activity for building a resume instead of a rewarding thing for its own sake. In the world of my-twelve-year-old-has-her-college-essays-done-already-what-can-your-child-do, parents sometimes forget that the journey is the point. A gentle reminder that their child is making progress and is happy can make a big difference.

Often, parents (usually mothers) who push their kids to ride are doing so because *they* want to be in the saddle themselves. These women were usually horse-crazy in childhood, but feel it's frivolous or selfish to start riding again. The only real solution is to get them riding, by hook or by crook. I always try the direct route first: "You sound like you're dying to ride, why don't you take a lesson this weekend?" If that doesn't work, I try the stealth approach: "You know, I really can't hold that after-school spot for Susie for the whole six weeks of soccer. Maybe you could take her place while she's playing?" As kids get older, use their growing social life to their mother's advantage: "Susie's sleeping over at a friend's house? Why don't you take her lesson this week since you're kid-free?" Or make a barn party out of it. One barn I know does Girls' Night Out lessons once a month, complete with margaritas afterward. Once they see other women doing it, they're often willing to join in and satisfy their need for saddle time.

6 Helicopter Parents

The opposite of the competitive parent, the helicopter parent wants 24/7 smooth sailing for his child: no criticism, unless it's done by the Oreo Method (compliment/criticism/compliment). 100 percent safety, 100 percent of the time. Always happy smiles, never any tears or frustration. And if it's not going perfectly, it's the trainer's fault. If you haven't dealt with one of these, you will; it's a cultural epidemic.

Rule Number 1: Do not placate or soothe helicopter parents. It won't work; they will simply find something else to fixate upon. Rule Number 2: Recognize that helicopter parenting is born out of fear; the Lizard Brain has run amok. These parents are constantly afraid: afraid of failing as parents, afraid of their children being hurt, afraid of their children being unhappy. This is a societal problem, not an equestrian one. It began in earnest after September 11, when we realized collectively that we cannot control everything. As a result, we started controlling everything we possibly could, especially for our kids.

There is no cure for this, because there's no such thing as 100 percent safe. The best you can do is show that you take all reasonable precautions, and that your teaching aims to increase students' safety by growing their competence, rather than by safety-proofing their environment. I explain that my school horses are trustworthy, but they are flight animals, so they will do unpredictable things. I refuse to say that a horse will *never* bite, kick, or buck. I emphasize that learning to hack and jump is safer than always keeping the pace slow and inside the ring, because sometimes the horse has other ideas. I try to demonstrate that the best thing to have in an unpredictable situation is a tool kit full of skills. Competence, not bubble wrap, leads to greater security.

7 "I Just Have a Quick Question...."

When you hear this opening line, you know you're about to have your riding time invaded, your dinner interrupted, or some other boundary crossed. Some students forget or ignore the fact that you are not available 24/7/365. They think that it's fine to call or text you on your day off because their horse is out of supplements, or to interrupt your ride to ask if they can have an extra lesson next week. If you call them on it, they always respond with, "But I just...." They see every request as minor. They also forget that while they are at the barn for recreation, you are there to do your job. Left unaddressed, boundary violations like this can leave you feeling resentful and disrespected, and the student feeling hurt because she doesn't know what she did wrong.

If you want a horse to stay in a paddock, you have to build a solid fence, maintain it, and remember to latch the gate. If you want people to respect your time and your boundaries, you need to set those boundaries clearly and firmly, and then *you must refuse to bend them* when someone pushes against them.

Do you always answer your phone or return a text, regardless of the time of day? When you are riding, do you stop what you're doing if someone asks you a question? Do you let people cancel a lesson an hour beforehand without expecting payment? If so, you are leaving the gate wide open for anyone to march through at any time. You can't really blame her when she does just that.

Clear, consistent policies are the simplest fences to maintain. Decide when your day begins and when it ends, and don't respond to any communication outside those hours. Just because your phone rings does not mean you have to answer it! Worried you'll miss an important call? That's why God gave us caller ID and voicemail. You can check the caller and the message immediately, then decide when to respond. If it's not a genuine emergency—a horse colicking or bleeding profusely—respond during your business hours.

If you are a compulsive message-checker, this may give you some panic attacks at first. You'll have to ride them out. They will subside once your Lizard Brain realizes that no one dies if you don't reply immediately. You will even discover that most of the time, people will solve their problems on their own.

Around the barn, limits can be more challenging. Everyone thinks their question is urgent and that "It will just take a sec." Explain that while you are riding or teaching, you are not available for questions or discussions. Emphasize that your horses and students need your undivided attention during that time, and that they are paying for that privilege. When you hear, "But I just," repeat yourself. People will grumble at first, but if you are firm, consistent, and clear, they will accept it eventually.

BE WILLING TO LET GO

Any time I talk about setting limits, saying no, or standing ground with a student, people worry, "But if I do that, they might go somewhere else, and I'll lose their business." Yes, that may be true: they might leave. But more often than not, they won't. And if they do, it might be the right thing for both of you. No single student is worth the sacrifice of your ethics, your training philosophy, your integrity, or the well-being of your overall program. Or, for that matter, your sanity. I've done this long enough to know that a student's departure usually feels like a disaster at the time, and yet it opens up space for something or someone new to come along. Be open to feedback and willing to change, but don't compromise your principles out of fear. Lizards have a terrible head for business—don't let yours make those decisions!

Any time you face a challenge with a student, ask yourself whether the Lizard Brain is taking over—your student's Lizard, or yours, or both. Learn to recognize it in its other disguises: anger, defensiveness, over-achievement, guilt, and shame. A grad school professor of mine once told me, "It doesn't matter if it's true, it only matters if it's useful." I've found it incredibly useful to assume that if someone is being difficult, it's because their Lizard Brain is afraid of something. With this assumption, I am much more likely to respond with empathy and calm than with my own fear and irritation. I'm far from perfect at it, but when I remember that assumption, things inevitably go more smoothly. We usually assume that our horses are doing their best; when we assume the same of our students, we can tap into their best qualities and bring out strengths they didn't even know they had. Happy teaching!

Final Thoughts

So here we are at the end, and ends are always just another beginning. I hope you've found the help you were looking for within these pages. In the wonderful tradition of Irish blessings, I send you and your sweet, sincere, over-protective Lizard Brain back to your horses with my own kind of blessing for you.

May you befriend your Inner Lizard, and appreciate how it protects and cares for you.

May you remember that when you don't feel okay, you can still be okay.

May your Lizard Brain learn that discomfort is not fatal.

May you speak to yourself with encouragement and kindness.

May you remember that you can do hard things.

May you spot a Brain Trap at a hundred yards, and find a path around its sneaky grasp.

May you invite a Committee into your brain that cheers you on and believes in you.

May you remember your skills when you need them the most.

May you find a state of Focused Calm in the midst of your stressful moments.

May your Performance Self be confident and strong.

May you recognize success, even when it comes without a ribbon or a trophy.

May you give yourself time and kindness when you need to heal from psychological or physical injury.

May you find the best possible equine partner for who you are and where you are right now in your life.

And above all, may you be well, may your horses be healthy and sound, and may you experience the greatest possible joy in this challenging, crazy, wonderful sport of ours.

Keep focused, keep calm, and kick on!

REFERENCES AND RECOMMENDED READING

Brown, Brene. (2012) *Daring Greatly.* New York, NY: Penguin Publishing Group.

Coyle, Daniel. (2009) *The Talent Code.* New York, NY: Random House, Inc.

Csikszentmihalyi, Mihaly. (1990) *Flow.* New York, NY: HarperCollins Publishers.

Emerson, Denny. (2011) *How Good Riders Get Good.* North Pomfret, VT: Trafalgar Square Books.

Gilbert, Elizabeth. (2015) *Big Magic.* New York, NY: Riverhead Books.

Gladwell, Malcolm. (2008) *Outliers.* New York, NY: Little, Brown, and Co.

Loehr, James. (1994) *The New Toughness Training for Sports.* New York, NY: Penguin Publishing Group.

Loehr, James. (2003) *The Power of Full Engagement.* New York, NY: Simon and Schuster.

Medina, John. (2008) *Brain Rules.* Seattle, WA: Pear Press.

INDEX